EXTINCT SPECIES OF THE WORLD

EXTINCT SPECIES OF THE WORLD

Jean-Christophe Balouet
Eric Alibert

Translated by K. J. Hollyman
English edition edited by Professor Joan Robb

BARRON'S

NEW YORK • LONDON • TORONTO • SYDNEY
in association with
David Bateman

First U.S. edition published 1990 by Barron's Educational Series, Inc., in association with David Bateman Ltd, "Golden Heights", 32–34 View Road, Glenfield, Auckland, New Zealand

All inquiries should be addressed to:
Barron's Educational Series, Inc.
250 Wireless Boulevard
Hauppauge, New York 11788

Library of Congress Catalog Card No. 90-35880

International Standard Book No. 0-8120-5799-6

Library of Congress Cataloging in Publication Data

Balouet, Jean-Christophe.
    [Grand livre des espèces disparues. English]
    Extinct species of the world/Jean-Christophe Balouet, Eric
    Alibert; preface by J.-Y. Cousteau; translated by K. J. Hollyman;
    English edition edited by Joan Robb.
        p.   cm.
    Translation of: Grand livre des espèces disparues.
    ISBN 0-8120-5799-6
      1. Extinct (Biology) 2. Nature conservation. 3. Extinct animals.
 I. Alibert, Eric. II. Robb, Joan. III. Title.
QE712.2.E97B3413 1990
575'.7--dc20
                                      90-35880
                                        CIP

PRINTED IN HONG KONG

CONTENTS

PREFACE

What a to-do over a piece of headgear! Because he refused to honor the Bailiff's hat, William Tell accepted having to take the worst risk a father can take. I hope my Swiss friends will forgive me, because I am only attacking a myth, one that goes against the traditional wisdom of their countrymen. Playing Russian roulette with a crossbow aimed at one's heir must indeed be the most criminal game of chance, the least heroic risk there is.

And yet in varying degrees the William Tell syndrome inspires most of the choices we make as a society. The young people of America will pay the crushing debt incurred by their parents. Our descendants for thousands of years will face the heavy cost of protecting themselves against the nuclear fallout and industrial discharges we are accumulating for them. Thousands of tomorrow's children will have to face up to limiting their own increase, sharing out resources that have become inadequate, and forging new moral values in a world of concrete and asphalt from which robins, rhinoceroses and butterflies have vanished.

In the meantime, we perfect, stockpile and distribute conventional weapons that are more and more lethal, we try to keep under control rockets that will bring about the end of the world, we multiply the number of potential Chernobyls, we eliminate hundreds of thousands of living species, we bore holes in the last atolls, and we heat up the planet at the risk of causing a flood without rain.

Children of the World, you each have an apple on your head.

Jacques-Yves Cousteau

FOREWORD

The evolution of humanity is closely linked with the evolution of animals and of the environment. Although hundreds of works have been published on human history, there has been no written account of natural species whose disappearance has been caused by man. Yet there was no lack of the necessary historical documentation. Cave paintings, hunting accounts, descriptions of the natural world, even cooking recipes and royal ordinances, offered material for just such a work. Marco Polo, Charles Darwin, James Cook, and many other early explorers encountered such species and described them.

Some species have become extinct more recently still, and the year 1987, for example, saw more than 50 of them die out. Drawings and paintings were made of them during their existence, and we have been able to find many of these documents. Their historical value and their quality are such that they have enabled us to make these species more familiar to the reader. The illustrations by Gould, Forster, Audubon, and Savery are genuine masterpieces.

Where the animals disappeared too long ago, or their disappearance passed unnoticed, we have used reconstructions. For these we have consulted the experts, sought out bone collections, and studied written accounts.

Our aim has been to present as many species as possible, particularly those with the most striking history, but we had no wish to produce an encyclopedia. We could not illustrate or even comment on each of the 600 lost species. Instead we have listed at the end of the book all the species known to have disappeared at the hands of humans.

A great deal of research was necessary, and documents in the National Library of France, the library of the French National Natural History Museum, and the National Archives, all in Paris, proved invaluable.

In some cases we decided not to include certain species whose extinction is not yet definitely confirmed.

While it is difficult to prove that humans alone were responsible for these extinctions, it is also often difficult to measure the influence of other factors — climatic change, for example. The role of humans has been the primary cause, in particular through hunting, but the introduction of predators such as dogs and cats, the destruction of habitats by fire, and the introduction of diseases or other competing species have greatly accelerated or complemented the human influence.

In an attempt to lighten such a serious subject, we have provided an abundance of illustrations and included a large number of anecdotes.

In order to ensure the book would be objective and become a reference work, we submitted the manuscript to many specialists, in particular research scientists at the Natural History Museum in Paris; the University of Paris; the Smithsonian Institute, Washington D.C.; the British Museum of Natural History, London; the Museum of Natural History, Madrid; and the Academia dei Lincei, Rome. We here thank those who helped us for their invaluable advice.

The Extinct Species

Humans have caused the extinction of innumerable species of animals. Because people hunted them; because dogs, cats and rats have continued to destroy them; because their forests were set on fire; because their feathers or their hides were worth more than their lives; because they were dangerous or merely nuisances; because humans wanted the trees they built their nests in or because their habitat was too wet, or would have made a good field or a good housing lot; because their flesh was delicate or even if only their tongues, tails, horns, teeth, livers or scales were sought after, more than a thousand species and varieties have today disappeared from our planet.

Well before the human species came on the scene, several hundred thousand species had already disappeared; our planet's history has been marked by many biological crises. There are many causes for this, and some of them may remind us of our present-day environment. A meteor shower, causing an atmospheric disturbance very like modern air pollution, may have caused the disappearance of the dinosaurs 67 million years ago.

The dinosaurs disappeared more than 60 million years before the appearance of the first humans.

Today the Earth has between 5 and 30 million species of animals and plants. Insects have the largest single share in this multiplicity of living things.

Care must be taken when declaring that a species has become extinct. Many species considered to have disappeared have been rediscovered a few years or decades later, sometimes in very small numbers. In fact, when environmental conditions become unfavorable, some species become greatly reduced in numbers and distribution, occurring only in refuge areas. These areas are often still largely unchanged by man, or even inaccessible, making it difficult to claim authoritatively that there are no survivors.

The discovery of new species confirms that we have not yet explored every corner of our planet. Madagascar, for example, which has a very high number of extinct and endangered species, very recently revealed a new lemurid, the golden hapalemur.

With plants, the disappearance of trees may not mean the extinction of the species. It is not uncommon to rediscover seeds many years later and to see them germinate.

Observations that are not confirmed by capture of specimens regularly cast doubts on the extinction of a species. This is the case with the Tasmanian wolf (a marsupial carnivore) and the diademed parakeet of New Caledonia. There is, therefore, an often considerable lapse of time between the last capture, the search, and the moment when extinction is declared.

Another difficulty for the naturalist who is specializing in extinctions is taxonomic validation. Binomial classification may be based on single

This 'jackalope' was just one of the many bogus animals created by taxidermists.

specimens, sometimes collected 100–200 years ago without the subsequent discovery of any others. It is then necessary to ensure that the known specimens were not hybrids, juvenile forms, or simply deformed individuals.

Some unscrupulous taxidermists and scientists have even amused themselves by inventing bogus species. The most famous example of this would be Piltdown man, but there are others that were purely frivolous, such as animals invented by putting antlers on a hare's head, or by gluing fur to a trout's body. Their inventors claimed, conveniently, that these species were rare or already extinct!

Often there is only written or pictorial evidence of recently extinct species. While such evidence bears witness to the imagination and skill of its authors, it does not provide scientific proof of the existence of the species. More than 50 species of vertebrates, in particular birds, are based only on descriptions by naturalist explorers of the 12th and 13th centuries.

Life is thought to have appeared on Earth 4 billion years ago. Physical and chemical changes together are considered to have been responsible for the creation of the first life forms, the bacteria. Since then the laws of Nature have produced a multitude of different living things. Some have conquered the air or the sea; some have reached a perfection that humans seek in vain to imitate.

The New Zealand takahe, *Porphyrio mantelli*, was rediscovered alive a century after the discovery of its fossil remains.

The Australian marsupials were seriously affected by the introduction of the placental mammals.

Definition of a species

The apparently simple question of defining a species has been answered in a number of different ways. Having the same morphological characteristics alone is not sufficient grounds for saying that two specimens necessarily belong to the same species.

The classification of living things, mainly established by Carolus Linnaeus (1707–78), is centered on the notion of species.

Today, we characterize a species in terms of a group of individuals or populations capable of reproducing themselves within the group and producing fertile progeny that resemble their parents.

Species are differentiated by their genetic inheritance, their size, their behavior, their adaptation to differences in climate or diet, their courtship display, etc., all of which help preserve the differences between one species and another.

The average time period over which a species exists, as determined from the fossil record, varies from 1 to 10 million years.

Species are grouped hierarchically into genus, family, order, class and kingdom, the aim of this classification being to reflect accurately their origins and evolution, and therefore their relationships. Different populations of a species also are often grouped into subspecies, races, or varieties.

The birth of a new species is today regarded as a biological event as natural as the extinction of another, but Nature cannot re-create an animal that has proved its own inability to survive. According to Charles Darwin, natural selection is the main driving force of evolution. The best-adapted forms survive; others, less adapted and less competitive, disappear forever.

Environmental changes, such as climatic variations or the arrival of new predators, have contributed greatly to extinction. Climates indeed have undergone major changes since humans came on the scene, but humankind has been the cause of thousands of extinctions. Historical records only confirm the human control of the environment. Hunting; destruction of the environment by fire or deforestation; the introduction of predators — these were to have much more disastrous effects than climatic changes upon the living world. Some experts are already forecasting the disappearance of more than 100 species a day by the end of this century.

Humans and Nature

Humans — like every other species — must be able to obtain certain specific elements from the environment in order to survive. Even though humans sometimes find their environment capricious, they take from it their oxygen, water and food, and the materials they need for their tools, clothing, and so on.

It is the lot of every living being to end up being consumed by others — whether it is eaten by a predator or consumed by scavengers or by bacterial decay after its death. Eating is certainly a need, and survival an aim. This rule seems to dictate every event in evolution and every kind of behavior. Thanks to the laws of Nature, many mechanisms of control seem to be established.

Humans seem to want to disregard Nature, and to believe in their ability both to do so and to dictate new rules. Sometimes humans seek their food with a contempt for long-established natural balances. Hunter and gatherer, the human species harvests according to its needs, even moving on to pursue

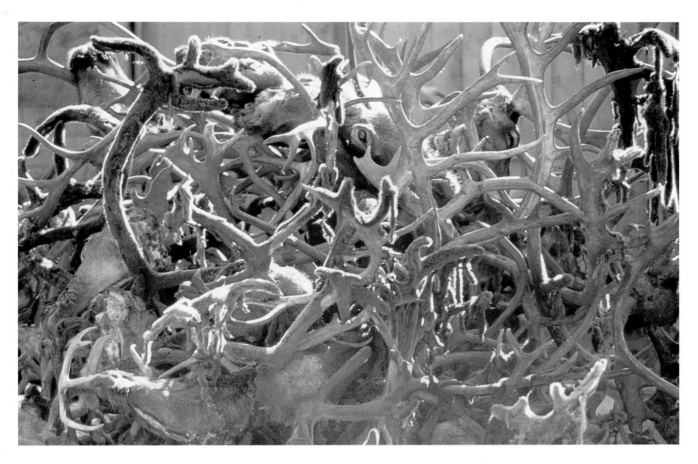

game. Following on the invention of agriculture and pastoral farming some 10,000 years ago, humans have tried to become free from the caprices of Nature, and to make Nature produce to answer their needs.

Edible species were rapidly discovered by humans, who selected those they found most enjoyable; and finding others a threat, they strove to get rid of them. Becoming aware of the uses that certain animals could be put to, humans domesticated them. Always drawing on the natural environment, the human species was rarely conscious of the future awaiting those beneficial species. Rare indeed have been the peoples who have thought of limiting their take from the hunt.

Anxious for economy of effort, humans used fire to hunt and to improve their environment in terms of their own needs. Thanks to technology, humans' independence from their surroundings kept pace with the growth of their needs. But they hunted, burned, and sometimes killed, when they did not have to. With the progress brought about by science, humanity thought itself master of all.

Recently, however, humans have become aware that they must conserve the sources of their food, but their ever-growing needs have often made them choose the easy solution, to the detriment of natural balances.

The devastating effects of fire in the urban habitat are well known; in Nature this is one of the most serious threats for species whose habitat area is reduced by it. The shepherd often follows a 'scorched earth' policy to encourage new growth in the pastures, to destroy parasites or 'noxious' species. Rarely is it recognized that this destroys species that are essential for the natural balance of the environment, and surrenders the land to erosion and eventual transformation into desert.

More than 100,000 reindeer had to be slaughtered after the Chernobyl disaster because they were so badly contaminated.

Through the ages hunting has been a prime cause of the extinction of species. (Painting by Gaston Phoebus.)

Bringing land into cultivation and building fences to control cattle are not compatible with the existence of migratory herds of large mammals. This has been a problem for the North American bison and the big African mammals that have been largely exterminated by landowners and poachers.

The predators, too, have been fought against without mercy. The hunting down of some of them, such as the wolves and bears, was declared to be a great national cause, and national coffers were opened to help eradicate these 'vermin.' The irony of fate has decreed that a few decades later costly measures have been undertaken to save the rare survivors — often too late.

The cortege of animals associated with humans comprises mainly the rats, the cat and dog, and the domesticated grazing animals. Although these species derive a large part of their food from proximity to humans, wild populations have also developed, drawing on the native species that are once again competing with them. Some of these species, such as the dog, cat, mongoose, and goat, were deliberately introduced into countries that had previously been free of them. J.R. Forster, the famous naturalist who traveled round the world with Captain Cook, wrote in 1778 that he firmly believed that, quite independently of the discoveries of land the expedition had made, it had done humanity a service by introducing goats to Tahiti, dogs to Tonga and the New Hebrides, and pigs to New Zealand

and New Caledonia. Unfortunately some of these animals became feral and within a few years caused the extermination of several dozen species.

Other species benefited indirectly from humans; for example, cockroaches established themselves in our kitchens and seagulls fed from our rubbish dumps.

Deforestation has today become a phenomenon of catastrophic proportions. Tree-felling initially allowed for the area of cultivable land to be expanded. Then the exploitation of timber as a raw material of prime economic importance became systematic. In Central and South America and Southeast Asia the reduction of forests is a major disaster. In the region of São Paulo the the area of forest declined by a mere 2 percent between 1500 and 1845, with the total loss of about 7700 square miles (20,000 square kilometers), but since 1907, 90 percent of all the forest remaining has been lost.

In the early 1980s it was estimated that the rate of disappearance of tropical rainforests amounted to 28.25 million acres (11.4 million hectares) per year, and that 41 percent of the world's original rainforest had already disappeared. It was predicted that, unless drastic action was taken, several Central American countries would lose all their forests by the end of the century, and all Indonesia's forests would be exhausted in 28 years. Sabah has recently taken action to stop logging in all primary forests, but the pillage continues unabated in Sarawak.

Today we are too close to the events to measure the exact effects of our newest technologies. The victims of our disasters at Chernobyl, Bhopal, and Seveso were human, but the effects on the whole world of living things

Each year bush fires destroy vast areas of vegetation in many countries of the world, thereby reducing habitat. This is the Chinese fire of May 1987.

were at least as great. Experts on pollution have great difficulty in quantifying the impact of such catastrophes on Nature, and their long-term consequences are therefore even more difficult to measure — for example, the loss of the entire herds of reindeer that had to be slaughtered after Chernobyl, and the millions of fish and seabirds that have been the victims of oil spills in various parts of the world.

The dingo, introduced into Australia by the Aborigines, has undoubtedly contributed to the disappearance of many species.

Humans have shown no indulgence toward their enemies, but for those species that caused no problems, humans have often shown little regard or much indifference because their role in Nature was not worth a war. The primary concern of humans seems to be the husbandry of beneficial species. A forecast today would suggest that nearly two-thirds of the animal and plant species without commercial value will disappear within the next century, whereas the species useful to man (the *anthropic* species as they are called) and the parasites should experience a population explosion.

Ecology, the biological discipline that is concerned with relations between species, enables us today to have an ever-greater understanding of these different factors. The knowledge gained enables the disastrous consequences of human activities for Nature to be summed up, but the authorities must obtain the means necessary to take action, and this is definitely not happening at present.

Other Causes of Extinction

Although the human species is usually the prime cause of recent extinctions, many natural events have happened, and still do happen each year, leading to major fluctuations in the population of certain species, and even in some regions to their disappearance. Climatic changes may be observed over years, centuries or 100,000-year periods. Their effects are most noticeable on small groups adapted to a limited geographical area and unable to find a refuge elsewhere.

The famous succession of ice ages during the Quaternary period seems, however, to have caused only a relatively small number of extinctions. In North America, where human settlement is comparatively recent (dating from 40,000 years ago), several waves of extinction have been uncovered and seem to correspond to the end of each ice age. These climatic vari-

The Little Ice Age was a long cold spell, lasting from 1645 to 1705.

ations forced populations to emigrate, but the only extinctions that can be attributed to them are the disappearance of a dozen species of large African mammals.

These variations, although numerous, are little understood by the general public, even though they have at times been quite major. The most remarkable was undoubtedly the Little Ice Age of 1645–1705, when for 60 years world temperatures underwent a major drop that has now been correlated with abnormally low solar activity. The resulting heavy snowfalls blanketed almost all Europe and North America. The effects on the fauna and flora are, however, still not well known.

The recent drought in Ethiopia, that was a disaster for many humans, caused some local extinctions, in particular of those species of migratory birds that usually wintered there. In the Transcaucasus, drought regularly causes the disappearance of the mole and the vole, and although these cases do not mean extinction for the entire species, or that the species will probably never return, they do illustrate the capacity of quirks of Nature to wreak havoc among her creatures.

Tropical ocean islands, where there are particularly many endemic species, have often suffered. The small numbers of individual animals, which can be explained by the smallness of the islands, have made them more vulnerable to disastrous weather. The great hurricane of February 27–28, 1760, in the Mascarene Islands caused a considerable fall in the bird population, as well as the deaths of 450 people. The worst hurricane on record caused the deaths of a million people in Bangladesh, devastating a large area in the Ganges Delta during November 1970.

Fires, some of them natural, contribute to the reduction or even the disappearance of species and of plant cover. In Australia, naturally caused bushfires have been so common throughout geological history that eucalyptus trees have evolved thick, non-flammable bark as protection against them. Fires there regularly devastate hundreds or thousands of square miles of habitat.

Sometimes when the decline of species is already well advanced, other natural catastrophes can destroy the last specimens. This was the case with The West Indian muskrat, *Megalomys demarestii*, the last survivors of which perished in the eruption of Mt. Pelée in 1902.

As a result of the 1902 eruption of Mt. Pelée, the already declining Martinique maskrat or pilori, *Megalomys demaresti*, became extinct.

Such natural disasters are believed to explain the extinction of species before the appearance of humans. For the dinosaurs, paleontologists have talked of a shower of meteorites, climatic change, variations in sea level, cosmic radiation, and other causes.

While it is true that several hundred animal and plant species have disappeared by human agency, this number has no common measure with the many millions of species that have become extinct since the first manifestations of life on Earth. On the other hand, international forecasts expect the disappearance of more than 100 species of plants and animals per day by the year 2050. This is a higher extinction rate than most biological crises have produced.

These forecasts, produced by the American group World Watch in a 1987 report, lead us to believe that the biological crisis of the 21st century will have consequences just as disastrous as the worst already experienced by our planet.

The Last Survivors

Many specimens preserved in museums are the last known representatives of extinct animals. Rare species have always aroused the interest of naturalists or hunters, and sometimes even been a reason to initiate research or exchange correspondence that has led to the discovery of dates, descriptions, and so on. Most of the information in this book is a summary of an enormous labor of research undertaken over nearly a century by hundreds of naturalists. Thanks to them, it is possible to retrace the history of the last representatives of some extinct species.

Paradoxically, it has happened on some occasions that the news that a species has become rare has led to its extinction, as 'collectors' rushed to obtain specimens for zoos, museums, or research institutions.

When the number of surviving members of a given species goes below a certain threshold (usually about 10), their extinction becomes almost inevitable. More than 100 species are at present surviving but their numbers are of this order or even fewer. Certain plant species are known by just a single plant and others even by one seed.

Where there are seeds, plant species can sometimes be revived even when there is no plant growing. This was the case with the dodo tree, *Calvaria major*, whose seeds germinated only after being eaten by dodos. After the extinction of the dodo, no seedling came up until in 1973 an American botanist, Dr. Stanley Temple, had the idea of force-feeding turkeys a few seeds. He was able to get three seeds to germinate — the first to do so for 200 years.

Certain species can be considered virtually extinct when a few specimens still survive. This is the case with the North American seaside sparrow, which disappeared in 1987; the last four known representatives were males. (See p. 156).

Localized disappearances, while not usually serious for the survival of the species, are often important advance indicators of future rarity and arise from the same factors as final extinction.

Zoos, private as well as public, have often accommodated the last survivors of species that are today extinct.

From 1600 on, one of the tasks of the great naturalist circumnavigators was to bring back for study the new animals they discovered. In many cases they did not even try to bring them back alive, but preserved them in alcohol or dried their skins. When they did try to bring live specimens home, these animals frequently would not survive the journey. Some of the specimens thus collected are the only ones ever known to western science — for example the two Society Islands parrots, *Cyanorhamphus ulietanus*, that Cook collected in Tahiti. No doubt a few more representatives of the species survived in their native habitat for a few years after Cook's visit in 1774, but nothing more is known of them.

When animals like these did survive their voyages, they were commonly placed in menageries. Unless a male/female pair had been collected, and both of them survived the journey, they could have no young. They became objects of curiosity for those in high places. The gardens of the Empress Josephine and the King of Bavaria possessed some birds that today figure among the rarest species.

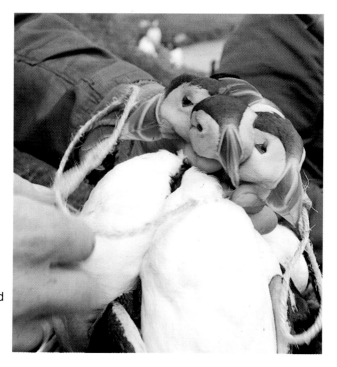

The distribution of the Atlantic puffin, exhaustively hunted by fishermen and a victim of oil spills, has been reduced by half in a century, and the bird has almost disappeared from the coasts of France.

This rarity should have led their owners to take great care of them, but curiously this was not often the case. The last known Tasmanian emu drowned in its owner's swimming pool, and the last recorded Syrian ostrich was killed by hungry German soldiers in 1944. Many specimens of other species died on board the ships taking them to strange lands far from their homes. Examples are a rat kangaroo, *Bettongia gaimardi*, which was killed by a ship's dog; a Falklands fox, which jumped overboard during a naval battle; and two dodos, which after being brought back to France, were served up in a sauce by the harbor master of Le Havre.

Conservation Problems

There are some special difficulties involved in keeping alive those species that survive only in small numbers. In most cases their rarity is the result of excessive changes in their environment. The ideal solution would be to preserve their habitats in their original state. Attempts to conserve species in their natural areas must therefore look to the eradication of introduced predators, the prevention of poaching, the provision of food, of help for sick animals, and finally the establishment of conditions favoring reproduction of the species in captivity — with a view to returning them to their natural habitat where possible.

In some cases the natural populations have entirely disappeared, and the only known survivors are safeguarded in zoos, as with the Przewalski horses.

Programs of reproduction in captivity are the key to the survival of animals whose wild populations we may be trying to re-create. This type of preservation needs populations of several dozen individuals and the

The Gallery of Extinct Animals at the National Natural History Museum in Paris has nearly 100 specimens of extinct species on display.

possibility of cross-breeding to avoid the effects of consanguinity. Even so, the chances of survival remain slim.

For the rarest plant species botanists have established conservatories. There are a few dozen throughout the world. In them seeds are stocked, and adult plants are regularly grown in order to produce new seeds to be shared out among the other conservatories or even replanted in the natural environment.

Unfortunately, when the species is approaching its final demise, biologists are completely without recourse. No one has yet tried to preserve the genetic inheritance of the most endangered species, whereas humans are able to freeze human embryos, the sperm of Nobel Prize winners, and even human corpses in the expectation that one day the progress of science will be able to bring them back to life.

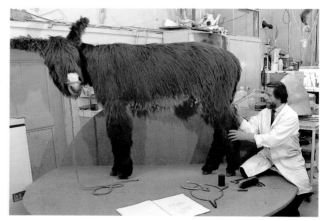

Stuffed specimens have to be preserved in a manner that will ensure they last for centuries.

Part of the stuffed animal collection of the National Natural History Museum in Paris.

For extinct species, the preservation of their remains should allow us to conserve this unique inheritance through the centuries. Light, dust, humidity, insects, and fungi are threats that can lead to early ageing or loss. Wars, too, cause the loss of dozens of unique specimens, e.g., when museums and other institutions are destroyed. Because of their rapid deterioration, one may wonder whether the stuffed birds and mammals in our museums will not end up as skeletons. However, here there is yet another sad irony; most stuffed animals do not even incorporate the animal's original skeleton! Usually their innards comprise only the stuffing material and an artificial supporting framework, with only the protruding limbs or skull bones incorporated.

Fossil specimens pose fewer conservation problems perhaps than specimens taken of live individuals. Several centuries or millenia old, only the fossil bones have been able to resist the effects of time. To save them there are advanced techniques relying on the most recent developments in physics and chemistry, but recourse to them is prevented by lack of time and money.

The only really effective solution is the preservation of natural habitats. They alone can guarantee the survival of species.

Selective Extinction

Just like the great biological crises that have marked our geological history, so the extinctions for which humans may be held responsible seem to have been very selective.

Ocean environments are as yet little changed, whereas land environments and especially island ones have already been profoundly modified. To date only one purely marine mammal, a huge sea-cow of the North Pacific called Steller's rhytina, *Hydrodamalis gigas*, has disappeared. However, recent evidence suggests a number of dolphins and small whales are now severely endangered.

Island environments are much more fragile than continental ones, because of the restricted variety of ecological niches and the small number of individuals living in a reduced space. Humans or introduced predators and competitors can very rapidly cause the extinction of most vertebrates, as well as other animals, living on islands.

Island-dwelling animals have suffered much from the human presence, but as far as we can tell the seas seem comparatively unaffected.

Birds are the first victims
of humans and cats.
Alectroenas nitidissima, of
Mauritius, died out in 1826.

Similarly, species restricted to unduly narrow or fragile environments, such as springs, dunes, and valleys, run the risk of disappearing with the first change in their habitat. Fires, floods, droughts, and the arrival of predators are further risks of extinction.

Mammals and birds are currently the main victims of human depredations on the environment. More than 1000 species and subspecies have disappeared to date.

Some groups, such as the crustaceans, although highly prized by gourmets throughout history, do not seem to have experienced any extinction for which humans can be held directly responsible. However, some land crabs are particularly sought after, and their numbers have undergone a genuine decline since the arrival of humans, while some species may have already disappeared.

Insects have often suffered from fires, especially on islands, and several hundred species are thought to have already been eliminated.

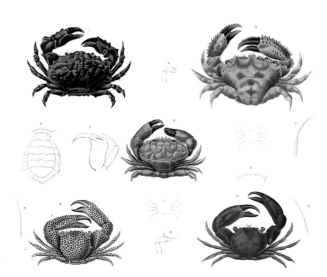

No crustacean is yet
known to have
disappeared as a result of
human activity.

It would appear the largest land animals are the first to go. Like flightless birds, many land species incapable of rapid movement are the special prey of humans and introduced cats and dogs. The only ones spared are those that have evolved some means of protection such as spines (porcupines and hedgehogs) or shells (tortoises).

In botany the problem of extinct species is quite different. Field research on vanished species results most often in the discovery of one or more seeds. Their longevity (300 years in some cases) is such that plant conservatories usually succeed in growing them. An example is the New Caledonian palm, *Pritchardiopsis jeanneneyi*, the heart of which was eaten by the convicts. One adult plant provided enough seeds for some 50 specimens now under cultivation.

Where human responsibility is clearly established, the list of reasons for extinction is headed by animals hunted for their meat, followed by those representing a danger or a nuisance.

To crown it all come the arbitrary choices that international organizations have to make in their safeguard programs. Lack of adequate funds means that they can manage only a fraction of the protection schemes Nature really needs.

The Extinction of Humans by Humans

The beginning of the Quaternary era, 2 million years ago, is marked by the arrival of the early hominids or human ancestors. Since then, several hominids have followed one another, and the appearance of each new species or subspecies has marked the disappearance of its predecessor. The first human was *Homo habilis*, whose oldest fossil goes back 1.8 million years. There were four species, all African. The last representatives of Australopithecus were to disappear 300,000 years after the appearance of the first humans. *Homo erectus* was to replace his African ancestors after some hundreds of thousands of years. *Homo sapiens*, who includes modern man, appeared over 600,000 years ago, followed later by Neanderthal man,

Neanderthal man may have been the victim of modern humans.

Queen Lijiwiji Trucannini, also known as Lalla Rooth, last of the Tasmanian aborigines, who died in May 1876.

and, about 40,000 years ago, by Cro-Magnon man. By a not altogether strange coincidence, this is also the time when Neanderthal man became extinct, and it is thought that *Homo sapiens* may have been responsible.

Paleontologists and prehistorians still debate the reasons for the disappearance of the species and subspecies of humans. We have much proof of the influence of climatic factors, but it would seem that humans' own responsibility was significant.

Many human populations have disappeared in more recent times. The extinction of the Tasmanian Aborigines is no doubt the most tragically

Lalla Rooth, die letzte Tasmanierin, † am 23. Mai.

well known. These island people, living to the south of mainland Australia, took fright at the arrival of the European expeditions of discovery, but subsequently showed themselves to be peaceful. The diseases introduced by the white colonists and the conditions in which the Tasmanian Aborigines lived brought about their disappearance. The last known individual, Queen Trucannini, nicknamed Lalla Rooth, died of natural causes on May 23, 1876, aged 76 years. The last Queen of Tasmania had been married five times. Her fifth husband, King Billy, the last Aboriginal male, had died in 1869.

In 1882 the French Navy surgeon C. Chauvin wrote:

> This race, recently extinct, is almost as unknown to us, in terms of its physical characteristics, as the races of old. The first colonists in Van Diemen's Land, more concerned about the prosperity of their settlements than with scientific studies, dealt with the natives only for the purpose of expelling them from their own territory, and firearms were used on more than one occasion, and not always as an isolated incident, to hasten a disappearance that the laws of Nature made too slow. Even the bones of these people are now rare; the small number collected have been sent to museums in England, as if to complete the dispossession of their soil by the inanimate remains of these first occupants.

Several other cultures have disappeared from the globe. A case in point is the Lapita people of the southwest Pacific, creators of remarkable pottery, and even more recently, the Arawak Indians of the West Indies, and Arctic peoples such as the Beothuk Indians of Newfoundland.

Why Preserve Species?

The species that have disappeared to date are certainly not the least interesting ones. Some provided such a source of food that they were hunted to the point of extermination. From the culinary accounts vaunting the delicacy of their meat, there is no doubt that these species would today have had high commercial value. Among them were many birds, such as the spectacled cormorant of the Bering Islands, various bushfowl and pigeons, Mascarene tortoises, and even the New Caledonian palm *Pritchardiopsis jeanneneyi*, which fortunately has recently been rediscovered and is being revived in cultivation.

The protection of species should not be considered simply as an act of generosity. The interest in their survival often goes beyond anything regional.

The chinchilla, *Chinchilla laniger*, would have become extinct but for the many farms established in its South American homeland and elsewhere.

Farming of the turtle *Chelonia mydas* on Grand Cayman Island. Breeding programs like these may save the species.

The green sea turtle, *Chelonia mydas*, held in particular esteem for both its meat and its shell, almost disappeared through intensive hunting and poaching of eggs. Today green turtles are protected by the Washington Convention, but the protection measures have in practice been less effective than the remarkable results of aquaculture. There are several such ventures in South America, Australia, and Southeast Asia with crocodile farming.

But species are not valued just for their effect on the palate. Others have been the object of big economic stakes. Sandalwood is a semi-parasitic tree of particular value in cabinetmaking, perfumery, and pharmacy; uncontrolled cutting of sandalwood on islands of the Juan Fernandez Archipelago in the Pacific put an end, around 1910, to a world market that, had it been better controlled, could today have provided an essential means of subsistence.

Certain species have had a high ethnographic or ritual value, like the eastern wapiti for its teeth, the Hawaiian mamo (*Drepanis*) and the Great

A crocodile farm in South America.

o-o (*Moho nobilis*) for their yellow feathers, and the New Zealand huia (*Heteralocha acutirostris*) for their skins as collectors' items. Their disappearance has put an end to many rites and traditions.

Furthermore, Nature functions as a whole, like a huge machine in which every part is indispensable. The existence of ecological chains is a reality we cannot ignore today, and many cases of chain extinction have already occurred, an excellent example being the case of the dodo and the *Calvaria* tree. (See p. 19.)

Many people do not think it worthwhile to protect dangerous species, but it has to be understood that like all others they are important links in the ecological chain. The destruction of North American mountain lions to protect deer, for example, caused great damage to the vegetation as the latter's unchecked numbers multiplied.

Each species living on our planet has its own genetic inheritance. The therapeutic properties of plants and animals are under continual study. Homeopathy and allopathy use many animal and vegetable elements. Chinese medicine, the sources of which go back several millenia, is essentially based on these kinds of therapeutic properties. Rhinoceros 'horn' (actually matted hair) is supposed to have aphrodisiac qualities and is also regarded as an antipyretic and antihemorrhagic. Tiger and panther meat are widely believed to be effective against muscular and articular pain, and whether or not these 'medicines' are pharmacologically recognized, the fact is that people believe in them and will go to any lengths to obtain them. Such people are unlikely to be at all concerned about the threat this poses to entire species.

The human species seems to set itself up as a supreme master, destroying what hampers it or seeking out what it needs or desires, without control or measure. Humankind plays at being the sorcerer's apprentice, and runs the risk of hastening its own end by destroying the balance of elements on which it depends.

Wastage

Few animals apart from humans seem to be characterized by wastage. The history of extinct species is very revealing from this point of view.

The extinct tortoises of the Mascarenes are a prime example; they were highly esteemed for their liver, which frequently was the only part eaten, the rest being left for the vultures. Even more thoughtless was the preparation of oil from the tortoise fat. An ax was used to make a hole in the shell of the living animal and a finger was inserted to see if the animal was fat enough. If not, it was abandoned as it was, and could not survive more than a few days. Animals considered fat enough were cut open and their fat was rendered down. Five hundred tortoises had to be butchered to get half a barrel of oil, without counting those that died — no doubt a similar number — from the effects of the 'test bore' in their shell.

The American bison was the object of wholesale slaughter by the American colonists. In some cases, only the tongue, which was particularly appreciated, was taken, the rest being left for coyotes and birds of prey. Pre-European Native Americans also used to cause immense wastage of bison when vast herds were stampeded into swamps or over bluffs.

Hundreds of thousands of wild animals are slaughtered each year, and their skins are sold as souvenirs in lieu of hunting trophies. As gifts they range from shoddy commercial products to valuables of great rarity.

The great auk, a major source of food for people, was wasted by being used as fish bait, and the North American passenger pigeon was used for pig food.

Crocodiles and baby seals, whose skins delight leather craftsmen, are dismembered where they fall, the meat being left to waste. Rhinoceroses and elephants, killed and stripped of their horns and tusks, are also left to rot where they fall.

The information gathered in this work seems to suggest that kings and politicians have favored, if not hastened, the end of many rare species. We may owe to some of these high-placed men a few effective measures favoring these species, but others have proved their talents as elite marksmen. The three specimens of the European bison (a particularly endangered species) housed in the Natural History Museum in Paris were hunted down by Napoleon Bonaparte, Napoleon III, and President Giscard d'Estaing.

Rarity seems to attract the well-to-do, primarily because, if you have the money, you can shoot at anything. Each year wealthy hunters go to the remote valleys of Afghanistan to pursue a very rare species of ibex; it costs them more than $3000. Others hire a helicopter to kill polar bears in Alaska.

Because rhinoceros horn is highly valued in the Chinese pharmacopœia, the animal runs the risk of extinction in the near future.

To produce wood pulp for paper, humans destroy hundreds of thousands of square miles of forest, thereby eliminating the habitat of many species that are thus condemned to extinction. Recycling of paper, that at present accounts for only a few percent of each year's production, could undoubtedly help conserve forests.

The deserts are another example of wastage. As most people today know, North Africa and the Near East were once covered in vegetation. Overgrazing, deforestation and bush fires are the main reasons for the spread of deserts.

Allowing species to become extinct is in itself a terrible wastage. Today time is running out for the most endangered species, and protection schemes are often urgent. Whatever measures are taken — legislative, financial or scientific — they will have no beneficial result if they are too late. One of the best examples is no doubt the Tasmanian wolf. In 1888, the Tasmanian government began offering a bounty for each animal killed; then, in 1938, it reversed this decision, deciding to undertake protective measures, but was too late.

History of the Protection of Species

The idea of conserving Nature already has a history. The oldest evidence we have is from Asia. About 242 B.C., nature reserves were created by the Indian emperor, Asoka. Marco Polo reports that Kublai Khan banned the hunting of certain birds and mammals during their reproductive periods. In South America during the reign of the Inca kings, seabirds responsible for the guano deposits were protected. Anyone going on to the islets when the birds were nesting or anyone killing one of the birds was liable to the death penalty.

The story of Noah's Ark for the first time puts forward the idea of humans taking on the responsibility of ensuring the survival of animal species. Noah did not seem to consider it possible to live in an environment devoid of animals. Moreover, the ark was designed to take in three pairs of each species, a number recognized today as the minimum needed to guarantee survival.

Today soil erosion follows deforestation, overgrazing, and fire, and leads to loss of the means of subsistence. The Chinese have known this for a very long time, as the 67th commandment of Taoism reads: 'Thou shalt not burn the pastures and the mountain forests.'

MÉMOIRE
Sur la deſtruction des Loups.

Les Loups ſont un des fléaux des plus redoutables dans les campagnes; on ne ſauroit imaginer les ravages énormes qu'ils y font, & il ſemble qu'on n'y a fait une ſérieuſe attention que depuis que leur rage s'eſt exercée avec fureur ſur un nombre conſidérable de perſonnes de tout âge & de tout ſexe.

La deſtruction de ces animaux qui, dans pluſieurs provinces, attaquent les poulains, les bœufs & les bêtes à laine, & en raviſſent un nombre prodigieux, ſeroit donc un objet d'autant plus eſſentiel que l'eſpèce des chevaux élevés dans les forêts & en plein air, ſeroit infiniment meilleure; que les moutons toujours parqués ſans danger, bonifieroient les terres, & donneroient une laine d'une qualité ſupérieure ſi l'on pouvoit ſupprimer les bergeries; & qu'enfin on préviendroit une quantité de malheurs dont l'humanité qui en gémit, n'eſt que trop ſouvent la victime.

Ce ſont ces réflexions ſans doute qui ont donné naiſſance à pluſieurs projets qu'on préſente tous les jours pour la deſtruction des loups; mais la plupart, ſous le

---

MEMORANDUM
on the Destruction of Wolves

Wolves are one of the most fearsome scourges of the countryside. They cause unimaginable ravages and it seems that serious attention has been directed to them only since their fury has been viciously wrought on a large number of persons of all ages and both sexes.

In several provinces where these animals are attacking foals, cattle and sheep and taking them off in prodigious numbers, their destruction is therefore all the more essential because the breed of horses raised in the forests and the open air would be infinitely superior; the sheep, always pastured out of danger, would improve the land and give wool of a higher quality if sheepfolds could be eliminated; and finally, a number of misfortunes would be prevented of which humanity is only too often the suffering victim.

These are the reflections that no doubt gave rise to the many projects that are put forward every day for the destruction of wolves . . .

DECLARATION
DE LOUIS XIII.

Concernant la Jurifdiction de la Capitainerie Royale des Chaffes de Livry Bondy.

Du neuf Juillet 1622.

LOUIS, par la grace de Dieu, Roy de France & de Navarre; à tous préfens & à venir. SALUT, fçavoir, faifons, parce que Nous avons été duement averti & informés que au préjudice des Edits & Ordonnances faits par nos Prédeceffeurs Rois, tant de fois réïtérés; plufieurs perfonnes de toutes fortes de qualités, même de condition des plus viles, qui devroient employer le temps à leur labourage, arts méchaniques ou autres, felon l'état & vacation dont ils font, fans aucun refpect ni retenue portent l'Arquebufe en nos Forêts, Buiffons & Plaines deftinés à notre exercice & plaifirs de la Chaffe, tirent impunément toutes fortes de bêtes fauves, noires, liévres, perdrix, faifans & toutes efpeces de Gibier, & y chaffent avec chiens, filets & engins, fi licencieufement, que nous fommes le plus fouvent fruftré de

---

DECLARATION
by Louis XIII
concerning the Jurisdiction of the Office of Captain
of the Royal Hunt of Livry Bondy
9 July, 1622

Louis, by the Grace of God King of France and Navarre, to all those present now and in the future, Greetings. Be it known that because We have been duly warned and informed that, to the Prejudice of the oft-reiterated Edicts and Ordinances made by the Kings Our Predecessors, several persons of divers qualities, even of the lowest rank, who should be spending their time in their ploughing, mechanical arts or other activities according to the state and service to which they belong, with no respect or restraint are carrying Harquebuses in Our Forests, Woods and Plains reserved for Our exercise and pleasures of the Hunt, are firing with impunity at all kinds of wild animals, boars, hares, partridges, pheasants and all kinds of Game, and hunt there with their dogs, nets and traps, so outrageously that We are most often prevented . . .

Some indigenous peoples have shown their determination to protect the species most useful to them, and that action no doubt goes far back. In the Hawaiian Islands, the feathers of certain birds were highly prized; killing them was therefore avoided, and the birds were released after the few feathers of interest had been taken.

An ancient representation of Noah's Ark.

For the protection of the aurochs, that at the end of the 13th century had become so rare they were found in only a few forests of Eastern Europe, Prince Boleslaus of Masovia forbade the hunting of them on his lands, and King Jagellon took even more severe measures a century later. In the 16th century, in an attempt to preserve the very few survivors, King Sigismund III of Poland set aside all the land the aurochs inhabited in the Jaktorov Forest as a reserve. Yet the species was to become extinct in 1627.

Until the 17th century all the measures instituted by kings and princes were aimed at retaining the exclusive right to the hunting of species that were rare or sought after. Louis XIII's royal ordinance (see p. 32) reveals these true motives for the limitation of hunting.

In the same way, the elimination of species that were terrorizing humans became a national cause. In France, wolf-hunt regiments were formed to flush out and kill the wolves. The state even posted up recipes for poisonous baits.

The first nature reserve was established in France, on August 13, 1861, on the initiative of several painters of the Barbizon School. It was at Fontainebleau, and covered nearly 1400 acres (565 hectares) of forest.

Three years later the American government set aside the Yosemite Valley in California as a national reserve. It was given the status of a national park in 1890. Yellowstone Park was created in 1872 with a view to offering the public a leisure area. South Africa set up the Sabi Game Reserve in the Transvaal in 1898, as a reserve for hunting game.

It was only in the mid 19th century that governments became aware of the need to protect Nature without getting any advantage from it other than the conservation of wildlife. *Man and Nature*, by G.P. Marsh, the first work on the protection of Nature, did not appear until 1864, in London.

The panda, *Ailuropoda melanoleuca*, is the World Wildlife Fund's emblem of protection of Nature.

Yellowstone Park, one of the world's oldest reserves, was created in 1872.

In 1895 the first international meeting for the protection of birds was held in Paris. It made changes of law possible in several countries. Then, in 1922, the International Council for the Protection of Birds was founded.

The first international conference for the protection of Nature was held in 1913, and the International Office followed in 1928. UNESCO in 1946 was responsible for founding what became the International Union for Conservation of Nature and Natural Resources (IUCN). In 1961 the World Wildlife Fund (WWF) was created by private sources. The Chinese panda was chosen as the WWF emblem, not only because of its great popularity at the time, but also to reaffirm the international character of Nature conservation, independent of political differences.

The Washington Convention of 1973 regulated trade in endangered species. Unfortunately, many countries have not yet signed this agreement, and often the means of guaranteeing its application are still not forthcoming.

Hunting has caused such ravages, especially since the invention of firearms, that detailed regulation and greater surveillance have become necessary. One of the most deplorable examples is no doubt the case of the polar bear, despite its hostile habitat, which one might have expected to discourage hunting.

If we look at the natural history of extinct or seriously endangered species, several conclusions may be drawn:

1. In the extinct or seriously endangered categories are, firstly, those species from which humans have drawn profit (tortoises, whales, etc.), except where humankind controls their reproduction and protects them against predators and disease (e.g., modern cattle); and secondly, those that have suffered competition or predation from introduced species. The causes of these extinctions (or the danger of extinction) include hunting, habitat degradation, competition with introduced species, etc. These factors have assumed alarming proportions that will not decrease in the future unless legislated against.

2. Not immediately endangered are those species that are particularly isolated or distant from areas of human influence. Fortunately that influence is still somewhat limited, but it is certain to expand with ever-increasing human activity.

3. Faced with the vastness of the problem, over a period of less than 10 years the main organizations for the protection of Nature have accepted the evidence that it is impossible to save all the endangered species, and have been led to make choices. Priority is given to the most endangered species, especially when they are the last survivors of families or whole genera, and also to those for which there is some certainty that they can be saved.

Finally, we may note that an important psychological change is taking place, giving the hope that many species can be saved, and that natural habitats will receive further protection despite economic interests and population growth.

Victims of Nature Conservation

In protecting seriously endangered species, a number of forest rangers and volunteers have lost their lives. Dian Fossey, the American woman who

Dian Fossey, who was murdered by poachers because she tried to protect the mountain gorillas of Central Africa that she had spent a lifetime studying.

lived among the mountain gorillas in order to understand them better and give them greater protection, was the victim of poachers. Other cases were George and Joy Adamson, the famous naturalists whose work was the subject of the book and film *Born Free*; both were murdered, in separate instances, presumably by poachers. In addition, many bloody confrontations between rangers and poachers occur every year in the African reserves.

Two rangers were murdered because of the fashion for egret feathers.

These murders are indicative of the stakes; the economic interests are great. The rarer the species, the more bans on hunting there are, and the higher the commercial value becomes. In Third World countries, measures for the protection of Nature are often seen as a deprivation, and indeed some peoples do in this way lose a source of food and sometimes substantial income. Measures dispossessing the peasants of their land, in order to protect the Caucasian bison, aroused their anger and led them to exterminate the last representatives of the species.

The protection of tigers in Southeast Asia poses serious problems of a different kind. In all, six subspecies of tiger are endangered; the Bali one is extinct. Where villages lie close to the edge of Nature reserves, unfortunate incidents are commonplace. Because the game that is its food is overhunted, the tiger, a carnivorous nomad, becomes starved and often leaves its reserve, sometimes becoming a man-eater.

Because the game that is its food is overhunted, the tiger often becomes starved and frequently leaves its reserves in India, sometimes taking dozens of victims each year.

Reviving Extinct Species

Because of the possibilities opened up by genetic engineering, research workers have indulged in the crazy dream of reviving extinct species. The most famous example so far is clearly that of the aurochs, the European ox that became extinct in 1627.

Lutz Heck, director of the Berlin Zoo, had the idea at the beginning of this century of crossing Corsican cows and Spanish bulls. Selecting those progeny that were closest to the aurochs, after 25 years he bred the first 'ersatz' aurochs, with spiral horns. His brother, Heinz Heck, who was director of the Munich Zoo, produced in 1932 a new race that was also very close to the aurochs. He did this by a crossbreeding program that involved the Corsican cow, West Highland cattle, the gray cow of the steppes, plus Holsteins and Anglers. Some descendants of these were reintroduced into the wild, where they subsequently redeveloped aggression and distrust of man. By 1984, the world stock of them comprized 72 males and 124 females. Today they can be seen in many zoos. However, they are not the true aurochs, whose genetic characteristics were certainly quite different from this artificially bred stock.

Cell culture in the early 1980s opened up the theoretical possibility of recreating an embryo from a cell. The Russians had the idea of reviving

The aurochs, *Bos primigenius*, disappeared in 1627. 'False aurochs' have been 'reconstituted' by the crossbreeding of European cows. A pair of such 'aurochs' is shown here in Gramat Park, France.

the mammoth from a cell taken from bulls frozen in the Siberian icesheet, using an ovum and the uterus of a female elephant. This made sensational news in 1982, but if the research was done the results are still not known.

Other attempts to recreate species by reverse crossbreeding have occurred for the Atlas lion, the Caucasian bison, the hemippus (Syrian wild ass), and the tarpan or wild pony of Europe and Asia. And as mentioned earlier, the dodo tree (see p. 19) was brought back from extinction.

It should be noted that despite the progress with genetics, it is impossible to revive an extinct species unless its genetic inheritance has been preserved in the form of cells. But even then there are many problems and no attempt has so far been successful.

The Indian Ocean
A Paradise for Birds

With an area of 12 million square miles (about 31 million square km), the Indian Ocean is endowed with more than 3000 islands. The main ones were discovered at the very beginning of the 16th century, when Leonardo da Vinci was painting the Mona Lisa and Rodrigo de Borgia was expanding his papal power.

Apart from Madagascar and a few other islands, the Indian Ocean was uninhabited and its terrestrial fauna was intact. First the Dutch, then the French, established several colonies there, with no permanent inhabitants before 1750.

The ships of the East India Company made many crossings and took the necessary provisions from the remarkable fauna. Land tortoises, present on most of the groups, were among the most prized, and played the part of "canned" supplies; they could survive more than 15 weeks without food or drink, and offered fresh, quality meat. These land reptiles were among the first protected species in the Indian Ocean, as early as 1671.

No marine species in this ocean is known to have disappeared in historical times. However, the Comoro region is well known as the last haven of one of the most famous living fossils, the coelacanth, *Latimeria chalumnae*. This very primitive fish was thought to have been extinct for 240 million years when the first specimen was brought to the attention of scientists in 1938.

But when it comes to the terrestrial fauna of the Indian Ocean, humans have eliminated more than 60 species. Among the extinct birds most recently discovered are a fossil duck and a rail, first collected on Amsterdam Island (French Austral Territories) in 1955. The fauna of the Maldives

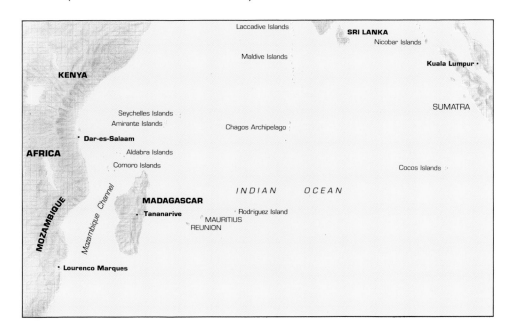

seems intact, but the most extinctions definitely took place in the Mascarene Islands, followed closely by Madagascar.

Unfortunately, the precarious situation of many Indian Ocean species is cause for deep concern. The lemurians are still hunted, and their meat is highly regarded by the Malagasies, especially when the animals have been fattened in captivity. The aye-aye, sole representative of an entire family of lemurians, has fortunately become regarded as sacred, and is now one of the top international priorities in the protection of Nature. The mesites, endemic birds on Madagascar, are known from a small number of individuals, and observation of them is very difficult. And at present only seven Mauritius kestrels (*Falco punctatus*) survive.

The Mascarenes

The Mascarene Islands were discovered by the Portuguese Diego Dias in 1500, and were then virgin territory so far as human settlement was concerned. Their mild climate and rich, exuberant fauna and flora evoked the Garden of Eden for the navigators. Hunting, and the introduction of rats, cats, dogs, pigs, and other livestock brought about the rapid extinction of 30 species of birds and seven reptiles.

Birds

The dodo, so dear to Lewis Carroll's "Wonderland", belongs only to a distant past. Little more than 200 years saw the disappearance of one of the strangest birds our planet has produced. It has now become a symbol of extinction. Hunted for food, it also attracted the attention of naturalists, and its world-wide reputation was well established when the last known specimen, from Réunion, died on a French ship returning home between 1735 and 1746.

Dried head of a dodo, one of the very few remaining relics of these extraordinary birds.

The Mauritian dodo, *Raphus cucullatus*. 'The longer they were cooked, the more insipid and tough their flesh became,' wrote Van Neck in 1598.

A 'Stupid Animal'

Sketch of a white dodo, made by Roelandt Savery in 1626.
During its lifetime, the dodo was often considered to be one of
Nature's mistakes. The descriptions have rarely flattered it, as
can be seen from the writings of Baron Grant, who was on
Mauritius from 1740 to 1758:

It is a thoroughly stupid animal . . . Its head is long, broad and
deformed. Its flesh is covered with fat but is also so nourishing
that three or four of these birds suffice to fill the stomachs of a
hundred persons.

'Lightness and activity,' wrote Buffon, 'are attributes proper to
birds, but the dronte [dodo] could not claim either of these
characteristics. It could in fact be taken for a tortoise covered with
feathers; and Nature, by decorating it with these useless ornaments, seems
to have wanted to add embarrassment to its natural ponderousness;
clumsiness of movement to the inactivity of its mass; and to make its
stupidity even more sickening by obliging us to admit that it really is a
bird.'

Curiosity spurred navigators and naturalists to try and bring examples back; some wanted to farm them, while others saw in them specimens of great interest for gardens and aviaries. Some were taken home to Holland, England, Genoa, Japan, and France, but conditions of transport were not exactly favorable on board, and many birds would refuse to take food or drink and died in captivity. Of all these specimens, all that now remains are a dried head and a foot in the Ashmolean Museum (Oxford), a foot in the British Museum, a head in the Copenhagen Museum, and various skeletons. Many bones have been collected since the dodo became extinct, along with many accounts and a few drawings. Its extinction had only just been recorded in 1801 when the Natural History Museum in Paris gave its taxidermy laboratory the task of modelling it in plaster and wax.

The bird was about 2½ feet (0.75 meters) long and flightless; it was gray, white or yellow; and it was also called dronte or solitaire as well as dodo. Three, or perhaps four, species lived on Mauritius, Réunion and Rodriguez.

The affinities of the dodo have been the subject of long controversy, and it took more than 30 years for the naturalists to agree on placing it among the pigeons. The ancestors of its family, the Raphidae, endemic

The white dodo of Réunion, or Réunion solitaire, *Raphus solitarius*, was solitary in its habits. It was the best game on the island, according to the explorer Dubois in 1674.

to the Mascarenes, are thought to have been on the African continent over 20 million years ago, when its ancestors were still flying.

The great French naturalist voyagers, Freycinet, Baudin, Dumont d'Urville, Bougainville, Laplace and Dupetit-Thouars came too late for the dodo, and were just in time to observe the last representatives of a dozen other species that are now extinct. Paleontologists discovered the remains of eight species not mentioned in any previous account. Their very recent age means we must regard them as having become extinct at the hands of humans.

The count of birds extinct at the hands of humans stands at seven species of parrots, three of pigeons other than the dronte, two of ducks, two of herons, four of rails, one grebe, one darter (*Anhinga*), six of nocturnal birds of prey, and one eagle. Four are known through stuffed specimens, the rest only by bones or even short accounts. The existence of some birds, like the giant waterhen (*Leguatia gigantea*) and two species of parrots, which are known only from vague accounts, was long doubted by the greatest naturalists.

Many writings tell of the abundance of these birds on the different islands, and the great ease with which they could be hunted.

> One finds there many birds, great and small, turtle-doves, parrots, etc., and a large species of bird the size of a turkey, so fat and with such short wings that it cannot fly; its feathers are white and it is not wild, indeed like all the animals on this island, none of them yet having been harassed or hunted. Ten men killed enough of them with stones or sticks to feed 40 people. (S. Castleton, an English resident, 1613.)

> We found here wood pigeons of the kind that has blue wings. They let themselves be taken in the hands, or we stunned them without their making any attempt to fly away. In one day we killed a good 200 of them. As we went further inland, we found a great many geese, wood pigeons, gray parrots and much other game . . . The geese did not fly away when we chased them . . . but what was

Fulica newtoni, an extinct rail from Mauritius.

Aphanapteryx bonasia, the Mauritian red rail, became extinct in about 1680.

most admirable was that, when one of the parrots or other birds we had taken made a noise, all the others of their species who were round about came rushing up, as if they had come to free it, and were caught themselves. So these birds by themselves provided us with what was needed to feed us. (W. Bontekoe, a Dutch resident, 1619.)

But the depletion of the wildlife made itself felt very quickly. As early as 1667, F. Martin, a French resident, wrote:

When some of the ships in the fleet were forced to set sail from the Mascarene Island by the hurricane that caught them there, there were many people left on shore whom we arranged to be picked up afterwards. During the time those people stayed on the island, they created an unbelievable commotion among the flocks, game and gardens. On Saint-Paul Pond, we saw no geese or waterfowl, yet earlier it had been covered with them.

The extinction of most of the Mascarene species took place during the 18th century. The three species of dodos were extinct on Mauritius in 1681, on Réunion in 1746, and on Rodriguez by 1790. The last specimens of Daubenton's starling, *Fregilupus varius*, were collected in 1840, and the last known specimen of the Mascarene parrot, *Mascarinus mascarinus*, was living in captivity in 1834.

Léguat's 'grouse,' *Erythromachus leguati*. 'Our grouse are fat all year and of the most delicate taste,' wrote Léguat in 1708.

ERYTHROMACHUS LEGUATI
(One-Half Natural Size—from a description and a drawing)

Reptiles

The extinct Mascarene reptiles include a small lizard, *Leiolopisma mauritiana*, two species of diurnal geckos, *Phelsuma*, and five land tortoises, *Cylindraspis*, endemic to the group. The tortoises were so large that in 1600 Admiral Verhooven said eight or nine persons could sit on the shell of one tortoise and eat their meal there. The first mention of these animals was recorded by Admiral van Warwyck in 1598.

In 1671 de Lespinay said the tortoises were 'so numerous throughout the island that one person could kill 1200 a day, or to put it more strongly, as many as he liked.' In 1708 Léguat commented on the abundance of tortoises on Rodriguez, saying there were sometimes groups of up to 3000,

Léguat's waterhen, *Leguatia gigantea*, lived on Mauritius. It is known only from Léguat's accounts of 1708.

Bourbon's hoopoe, *Fregilupus varius*. The last four known specimens were captured in May 1835, but escaped a few months later.

'The tortoise is a very ugly animal...but very good eating,' wrote Carpeau du Saussay in 1666.

so that it was possible to take more than a hundred paces on their backs without setting foot on the ground. 'In the evening they gather in cool places and get so close to one another that the area seems to be paved with them.'

It is estimated that from 1732 to 1771 the number of tortoises slaughtered on Rodriguez alone was about 280,000. Their meat was used in the butchery trade and in medicine, but also to feed pigs or in exchange for poultry. When the scarcity of the tortoises became too noticeable, there

$\frac{2}{3}$

was an organized traffic in them from Madagascar to the Seychelles through Aldabra.

Because of the slaughter and wastage, and in order to preserve species that were very useful for provisioning ships, measures of protection were taken with due speed. The first ordinance aimed at protecting the tortoises was dated May 12, 1671. A decree of 1710 limited the take to six tortoises a year per person, with a ban on taking young. A royal ordinance of 1715 established the punishments and fines that could be handed out to those contravening the regulations; $16 for whites and 100 strokes of the whip for blacks. The extinction of these endemic tortoises occurred on Mauritius in 1735, on Rodriguez in 1804 and on Réunion in 1840.

The Mascarene parrot, *Mascarinus mascarinus*. Of the three specimens known, only two have been preserved; the third lived until 1835 in the King of Bavaria's menagerie.

49

Madagascar

The diversity and uniqueness of Madagascar's fauna make this largest island in the Indian Ocean one of the most remarkable sanctuaries on Earth. Inhabited by humans during the first millenium of our era, its fauna had become greatly impoverished by the time the first voyagers arrived at the beginning of the 16th century. Some 20 species of vertebrates had disappeared, and the majority of those still surviving are among the least well known or the most endangered.

The extinction of a sizable proportion of the Malagasy fauna was caused by hunting, but bush fires brought about the destruction of a major part of the forest cover that sheltered its large animals.

Birds

As on some other large islands such as New Zealand, there was a rich fauna of giant flightless birds. There were seven species of these, and the largest, *Aepyornis maximus*, was over 10 feet (3 meters) tall. Along with the giant birds of New Zealand, these were the largest land birds ever known. Because they were so massive, the Malagasy forms were no doubt the heaviest. Prodigiously robust, they were nicknamed 'elephant birds'. Their extinction, as the result of hunting, is thought to have occurred at the beginning of the 17th century.

The western world's first tangible proof that these birds existed was the discovery of a giant egg in 1851. It measured nearly 13 by 9 inches (34 by 24 centimeters), had a volume of nearly 2 U.S. gallons (7.5 liters), and greatly impressed naturalists who saw it. In Malagasy, the bird's name is *vorompatra*. There can be no doubt that these birds were hunted for

The *Aepyornis* egg discovered in 1851. Such eggs measured up to 13x9 inches (34x24 centimeters) and had a volume of nearly 2 US gallons (7.5 litres).

their flesh, as many of the bones found since show the marks of cutting tools. Among the pottery deposits, carved bones and even a hair were found. Two fossil tibias collected in 1900 had had two holes pierced in them by human hand, although the purpose of this remains unknown. These observations show the close links there were between humans and the big birds. From 1850 many surveys were organized to try and find the giant birds, but without success.

Bones of at least three other species of extinct birds — a rail, a duck and a goose — have been discovered in the same deposits, but there is good reason to think that a far greater number of birds existed that remain unknown to us, because only the largest bones have been collected and studied. It appears also that a description of at least two other species of birds, including a pigeon, will shortly be made. The revision of the Malagasy subfossil fauna and further excavations may also have a few surprises in store.

Delalande's cuckoo, *Coua delalandei*, is known only from a few specimens dating from the mid-18th century.

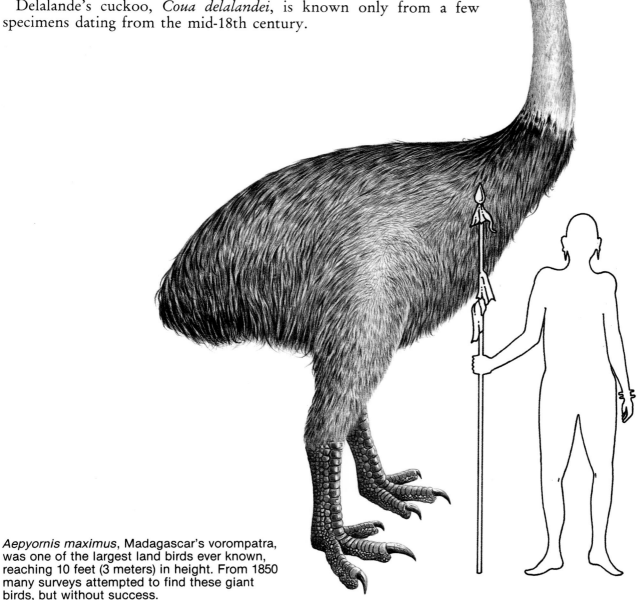

Aepyornis maximus, Madagascar's vorompatra, was one of the largest land birds ever known, reaching 10 feet (3 meters) in height. From 1850 many surveys attempted to find these giant birds, but without success.

Trybonyx roberti, an extinct
rail of Madagascar.

Marco Polo and the Roc
Marco Polo, the famous Venetian traveller who crossed the Indian
Ocean at the end of the 13th century, tells in his chapter on
Madagascar and Zanzibar the story of a giant bird:
The people of the island report that at a certain season of the
year, an extraordinary kind of bird, that they call a rukh [roc],
makes its appearance from the southern region. In form it is said
to resemble the eagle, but it is incomparably greater in size, being
so large and strong as to seize an elephant with its talons, and
to lift it into the air, whence it lets it fall to the ground, in order
that when dead it may prey upon the carcass. Persons who have
seen this bird assert that when the wings are spread they measure
sixteen paces in extent, from point to point, and that the feathers
are eight paces in length, and thick in proportion.
Sinbad the Sailor is said to have seen an egg coming from a bird
of incredible size.
   These descriptions seem at first sight to correspond to *Aepyornis*,
but the roc's powers of flight and the supposed presence of the
elephants raise doubts. The roc may perhaps instead have been
a giant bird of prey, also extinct, that lived alongside herds of
dwarf elephants in the Mediterranean.

Coua delalandei, an unusual bird known as
Delalande's cuckoo, was recorded from a single
specimen retrieved in Madagascar in the 1850s.

Reptiles

As on the Mascarene Islands, the tortoises suffered greatly from human presence, that regrettably led to the extinction of two giant species. The shell of the largest species, *Dipsochelis grandidieri*, was more than 4½ feet (1.4 meters) long.

An endemic subspecies of crocodile was discovered in 1872 among fossil remains. The neighboring Seychelles used to have a species of tortoise, *Dipsochelis daudini*, which became extinct during the 19th century. One young specimen of it is housed in the Paris Natural History Museum.

Three Seychelles Islands turtle species are also extinct.

This tortoise of the Seychelles, *Dipsochelis daudini*, became extinct in the 19th century.

Mammals

Among the extinct mammals are two species of hippopotamuses. Vague legends speak of a water buffalo (in Malagasy called *omby rano*), that in all probability really corresponds to these pachyderms. From these accounts, they may have survived until the beginning of this century. They were small — only about 7 feet (2.1 meters) long and about 3 feet (1 meter) high. Monkeys, tortoises, and birds in Madagascar were mostly giant forms, and these are thought to have been the only pygmy animals there.

At least three species of rodents are thought to have died out, but the extinction prize for Madagascar must go to the lemurians. Apart from a few African and Indo-Malayan species, present-day forms are strictly localized in Madagascar. These archaic simians in earlier times included

One of the big Malagasian lemurians, *Megaladapis*, is thought to have survived until the 17th century. Only bones of these large species of archaic simians give clues to their existence.

several large species. Although some of these have been described as 'giant,' in fact their sizes have frequently been exaggerated. *Magaladapis* must have measured about 6 feet (2 meters). Its skull is 12 inches (30 centimeters) long, presenting an elongated face ending in a snout. Its nearest known relative lived 40 million years ago — in the Paris Basin.

Another big Malagasy primate was described by Flacourt in 1652:

> Tretretretre, or Tratratratra, is an animal as big as a 2-year-old calf with a round head and a human face; the front feet are like a monkey's, and the hind feet too. Its hair is crimped, its tail short, and its ears like a man's. It is like Ambroise Paré's thanacth . . . It is a very solitary animal; the people of the country are very frightened of it and run away from it just as it does from them.

This fear the Malagasies felt when facing these big animals prompts us to look for some reason other than hunting to explain the disappearance of the big simians. Forest fires caused the land to dry up and brought about a big decrease in the forest cover, thereby reducing the habitat of these animals. The last of them may well have been devoured by dogs during the 17th century.

The North Pacific
From James Cook to the Battle of Midway

Pacific island fauna is characterized by an absence of indigenous mammals apart from bats, and by an abundance of birds and lizards. However, almost half the recorded animal species are now only known from their fossil remnants.

Research continues to uncover the existence of species, usually large in size, whose disappearance was brought about by the first human inhabitants of the islands. Hunted for their feathers or their flesh, or by introduced predators, the birds were the prime targets. The reptiles, and particularly the lizards, suffered greatly from being hunted, but the study of their remains has been so limited that it is impossible to make any final assessment. The number of extinct bird species — more than 100 — is purely provisional, and could in the next few years be doubled or trebled.

Habitation of the major islands by humans goes back nearly 3000 years. In certain groups, such as Vanuatu, the introduction of dogs and pigs took place very early. Elsewhere, their introduction by the 18th-century explorers added a further dimension to the threat already looming over several hundred indigenous species, and hastened their extinction.

Captain James Cook was the greatest pioneer explorer in this ocean, making in all three voyages of exploration. On each voyage he was accompanied by naturalists who made many important discoveries. His 1768 voyage, arranged by the Royal Society of London, had as its mission the observation of the transit of Venus, in order to calculate the distance from the Earth to the Sun.

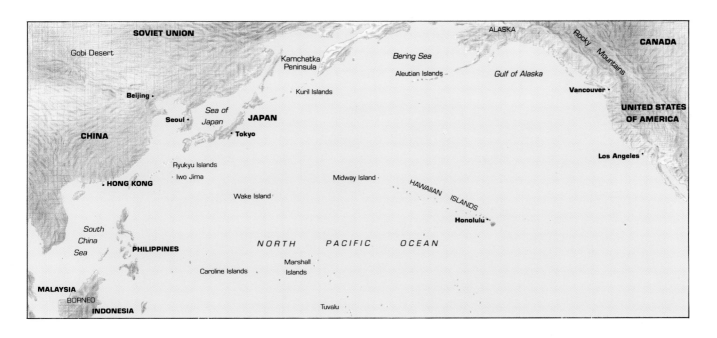

Bering Island

Bering Island bears the name of the unfortunate captain of the *St. Peter* that was wrecked there in 1741. Among the survivors was a young naturalist, Georg-Wilhelm Steller, who realized there were two endemic species; a gigantic sea cow, *Hydrodamalis stelleri*, and the spectacled cormorant, *Phalacrocorax perspicillatus*. Conditions were very difficult; there was no shelter and hardly any wood to light a fire. For food, the shipwrecked crew hunted seals, the sea cow, and the cormorants.

Steller's sea cow was even bigger than the manatees and dugongs, which are today the only survivors of the Sirenia family, and are protected by international law. The survivors of the *St. Peter* had the privilege of eating the flesh of this peaceful marine mammal that lived in herds in the shallow waters around Bering and Copper Islands and fed on seaweed. It grew to 30 feet (9 meters) in length, and the largest individuals weighed nearly 6 tons. Their nearest living relatives are not the whales or seals, but the elephants. Their meat was very delicate, and some even considered that it was 'superior in quality to beef and, when correctly prepared, made an acceptable substitute for corned beef.'

The sea cows were hunted not far offshore, with harpoons attached to a strong rope held by up to 40 men on the shore. It seems that several hundred individuals were hunted in this way. In the 27 years following their discovery, the species became extinct.

In the description Steller gave of this mammal, he provided extensive details on its mating and parental behavior:

> In spring they mate like human beings, particularly at the end of the day when the sea is calm. Before they come together, long erotic foreplay takes place. The female, followed constantly by the male, swims tranquilly, coming and going, avoiding him by many roundabout means, until, impatient, she turns on her back as though

The Japanese sea lion,
Zalophus californianus japonicus.

worn out and conquered, and the male rushes violently on to her, pays the tribute of his passion, and they give themselves to each other in a mutual embrace.

The Bering Island cormorant, that weighed up to 15 pounds (7 kg), was very edible game, even though the bird fed on fish. The castaways prepared it gypsy fashion, whole with the feathers intact, encased in clay and cooked in embers. For a long time this cormorant was known only through Steller's account. The first specimen was collected in 1837, and the species was extinct by 1850.

Steller's sea cow, *Hydrodamalis stelleri*, was presumed extinct just 27 years after its discovery in the North Pacific in 1741. The species was even bigger than the manatees and dugongs that are now the only survivors of the Sirenia family and are protected by international law.

In 1741 the spectacled cormorant of Bering Island was hunted by the shipwrecked crew of the *Saint Pierre*, and cooked over an open fire. The first specimen was collected in 1837; the species was extinct by 1850.

Hawaii

Discovered on Christmas Day 1777 by Cook, the Hawaiian or Sandwich Islands already had an impoverished fauna. This was true of the birds, more than 40 species of which are today extinct, and also of the plants and insects. More than 80 percent of the forest has now been destroyed by fire, grazing, and agriculture, so that 300 species and varieties of plants are said to have already vanished, while 800 others are endangered. A species of hibiscus, *Hibiscadelphus wilderianus*, is thought to have disappeared at the end of last century. Related species, saved by cultivation, have been reintroduced on the slopes of the volcano on Hawaii Island.

The Sandwich rail, *Porzana sandwichensis*, became extinct in 1884. It apparently had the habit, when threatened, of taking refuge in burrows dug by rats, which led to it surviving only a few decades after their introduction.

Another endemic rail, *Porzana palmeri*, that lived on Laysan Island, east of the main Hawaiian group, disappeared in 1944. This island was inhabited by Europeans from 1828 on, especially for the exploitation of guano. Rabbits were introduced in 1903 and destroyed the rail's habitat. In 1911 there were still 2000 rails there, but none by 1920. The species survives only on the neighboring Sand and Eastern Islands, where they were introduced in 1891 and 1910, respectively. After the rabbits were exterminated from Laysan in 1924, no one seems to have thought of reintroducing the rail to its original island, which would have ensured its survival. They were lively birds, and not afraid of man. At the beginning of World War II they were even seen round the military camps, scavenging food scraps.

Hibiscadelphus giffordianus was known only from one specimen in the wild that died in 1930. It was, however, saved by cultivation, and 12 plants now exist.

In 1943 a ship ran aground on Midway and its rats invaded the island. The last rail was seen in November 1943 on Sand Island, and in June 1944 on Midway.

Flightless geese, *Thambetochen*, lived on the main islands of the Hawaiian group. There were seven species, which have all disappeared, hunted by the Polynesians, and only their bones remain today. Most of the specimens are of recent origin, and are still being studied and described. The birds show a wide range of beak forms, which is characteristic of highly specific food diets, but they also show quite unusual skeletal characteristics, reminiscent of large flightless birds like the ostrich, and so show a most remarkable convergence of form.

A flightless species of ibis was rediscovered in fossil deposits.

In the lists of extinct Hawaiian birds, that of the passerines is particularly long. Their feathers were used to make capes and headbands, and to ornament chiefly helmets or *mahiole*. The red feathers, which were the most plentiful, were less prized than the yellow ones reserved for the great chiefs. These latter were provided by two species; *Drepanis pacifica* (a finch) and *Moho nobilis* (a honeyeater), both extinct today. Each bird produced only about 10 of these feathers.

Cook wrote in 1778:

> In war or on occasions of state the Chiefs are dressed very elegantly in red-feathered Caps and Cloaks. The Caps are made of wicker work . . . and are covered with red and yellow feathers . . . The Cloaks are made of fine Netting with red and yellow feathers curiously worked upon them; these they have of various Lengths, some coming no lower than the waist and others trailing the Ground. A more rich or elegant Dress than this, perhaps the Arts of Europe have not yet been able to supply.

In his new collection of plates in 1838, the naturalist Temminck wrote of *Moho nobilis*:

> The most striking characteristic of this species is a tuft of beautiful long silky feathers decorating each flank; the bright yellow colour

One of the two extinct flightless ibis of Hawaii, where to date more than 40 species of birds have disappeared.

The yellow and red feathers of Hawaiian passerines were used for making headgear and capes for chiefs.

The Hawaiian honeyeater or moho, *Moho nobilis*, produced only about ten of its distinctive yellow feathers, and these were reserved for the ornaments of great chiefs. This painting by Temminck was published in 1838.

of this waving plume makes a pleasing contrast to the otherwise dark colouring of its plumage. These are probably the feathers Sandwich Islanders use to make their red cloaks bordered with yellow. The English traveler Dixon tells us they catch these birds with ease, pull out the bunches of feathers on the flanks, and then let the birds go.

Gaimard, naturalist on the *Uranie* and *Astrolabe* expeditions, remarked: When we think that to make one of these cloaks, and they are sometimes five feet [1.5 meters] long, hundreds and maybe thousands of these birds are needed, our astonishment is doubled not to see one of the birds at every step; yet the French navigators did not see a single one on the three islands of Ouhyhi, Moawi and Wahou & Hawaii, Maui and Oahué. We must believe that the numbers ended by being so diminished that the birds now find themselves relegated to the deep valleys or the very high mountains of the interior.

About 1825, natives paid one Spanish dollar for five of these feathers. There are no yellow birds now in Hawaii, the last of them having disappeared around the 1850s.

Hawaiian honeyeaters belonged to five species, only one of which still survives on the island of Kauai where its continued existence is at risk. Fewer than 10 specimens have been recorded at census. The name of this bird was *o-o*. The Oahu o-o, *Moho apicalis*, is thought to have become extinct in 1837, Bishop's o-o from Molokai, *Moho bishopi*, in 1904, and the Great o-o of Hawaii, *Moho nobilis*, in 1934, but these species may be rediscovered. Their disappearance seems to have been hastened by the action of cattle on their environment, but above all it is evident that they were widely hunted by cats. In 1892, the remains of 22 of these birds, killed by cats in less than two days, were discovered in one valley on Lanai Island.

Vestiaria coccinea provided red feathers for ornaments. Painting by William Ellis, 1774.

The Drepanididae are a family of finches endemic to Hawaii. Less than a century ago there were nine genera and 22 species. Today three genera, nine species, and 18 subspecies have become extinct. The Oahu akepa *Koxops coccinea rufa* lived on Oahu; the last known specimen was captured in 1893. The Molokai Alauwahio *Paroreomyza maculata flammea*, of Molokai, disappeared in 1937. The great amahiki *Viridonia sagittirostris* died out in 1900. The greater Koa finch *Psittirostra palmeri* lived on the slopes of the Mauna Lao volcano. It seems to have disappeared about the end of last century. The lesser Koa finch *Loxioides flaviceps*, which lived on several islands of the group and was a dwarf in comparison with its related species, was last observed in October 1981. The Kono finch *Loxioides kona*, the smallest of these finches and an inhabitant of several islands, was last sighted in 1894.

A Hawaiian chief's feather hat or *mahiole*.

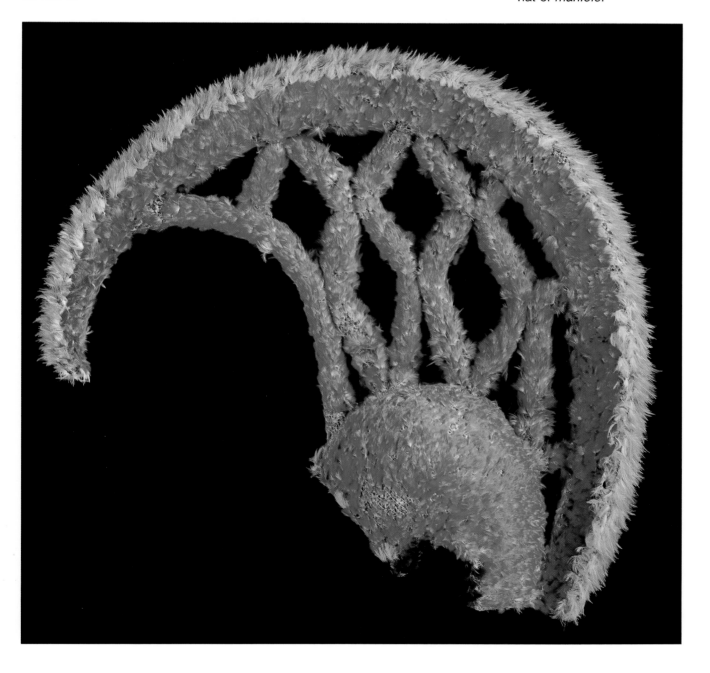

Extinct Hawaiian passerines.

Like the Galapagos finches studied by Darwin, these passerines evolved very rapidly and independently on each of the islands, and adapted themselves to different ecological niches and dietary regimes. The most specialized birds apparently suffered the most severely from the introduction of predators and competitors. Many new diseases against which they had no resistance, such as malaria, were introduced. Mosquitoes, the main carriers of many bird diseases, including malaria, colonized the islands from 1826 on. The introduction of cattle and predators such as cats combined their effects, and in less than 150 years these remarkable species were eliminated.

On Washington Atoll there was a subspecies of duck, the gadwall, *Anas strepera couesi*, that was no larger than a teal. It was discovered in 1874 by a U.S. Navy surgeon, but no more have been found since.

Bonin Islands

In 1827, a naturalist from the British ship *Blossom* visited the Bonin Islands, lying 440 miles (700 kilometers) south of Tokyo. He found rats and pigs were plentiful there because of many previous shipwrecks. In 1853 the Bonin fauna was already much impoverished and today the extinction of a pigeon and a heron is recorded, the result of rats and hunting by humans.

The human population remained low until 1900. From 31 persons in 1853, it rose to 100 in 1875, then to more than 5000 in 1900, after annexation by Japan in 1875.

The Bonin black or shining pigeon, *Columba versicolor*, was still plentiful when the island was discovered, but not in evidence after 1900. The last known specimen was killed in 1889 on Nakondo Shima. Ten years earlier, on this same island, the last specimen of *Nycticorax caledonicus crassirostris*, an endemic subspecies of the rufous night heron, was collected.

The Bonin subspecies of rufous night heron, *Nycticorax caledonicus crassirostris*.

Wake

Isolated in the Pacific north of the Marshall Islands, Wake was the site of very heavy fighting during World War II. Although its occupation by the Polynesians was already of long standing, there was still one land bird left, the Wake Island rail, *Gallirallus wakensis*, when Japanese troops set up camp there in 1945. Needing food, the soldiers killed and ate all the rails remaining on the island.

The Wake Island rail, *Gallirallus wakensis*, was finally exterminated by Japanese soldiers in 1944.

Carolines

The Caroline Islands also had a small rail, *Porzana monasa*. Two birds were collected in December 1827 by von Kittlitz, naturalist with the Russian explorer Senyavin. They are the only known specimens of this species, which disappeared about 1870.

A starling endemic to Kusaie Island, *Aplonis corvina*, survived only a short time after the collection of five specimens by von Kittlitz in the same year. This forest bird was no doubt eliminated by rats.

Iwo Jima

The island of Iwo Jima, south of Japan, had a further rail, an endemic subspecies, *Poliolimnas cinereus brevipes*. These little crakes, 6 inches (15 centimeters) long, lived in the forests of the island until their almost total destruction. The last specimen was collected in 1911, and the last observations made in 1924. Various other subspecies of this crake exist in the Pacific, but they are in general all close to extinction.

The extinct rail of Iwo Jima. It did not survive the destruction of its habitat, a likely fate for many other subspecies of this crake living on islands in the Pacific.

Guadalupe

The Mexican island of Guadalupe, situated 140 miles (225 kilometers) off the Californian coast and dominated by a mighty volcano, is today inhabited by tens of thousands of sheep and feral cats, and not even half the original species survive.

The Guadalupe Island petrel, *Oceanodroma macrodactyla*, like most storm petrels, nested in cliffs. The single chick was fed by its parents that spent the day at sea. It is doubtful that the members of the colony were never very numerous. The introduction of cats condemned them, the chicks being killed in their nests. This species became extinct about 1911.

The story of the caracara, *Polyborus lutosus*, is especially tragic. This large flightless bird of prey, related to the falcons but looking more like an eagle or vulture, fed on carrion, rodents, insects, and worms. Because some farmers claimed that it also killed young lambs, they waged war on it mercilessly. It was regularly shot by hunters, and poisoned baits hastened its destruction. Twelve specimens were collected in 1875. By 1879 there were only seven left, and a goat-hunter caught four alive that he sold. The Smithsonian Institution in Washington (assuredly the world's greatest naturalist body) apparently suggested buying them for $100. Another offer of $150 per bird was made to the owner of these very rare specimens. He delayed too long in making the sale, and the four birds died a few months later.

The caracara, *Polyborus lutosus*, of the Mexican island of Guadalupe. The last observation of this large flightless bird of prey was made in December 1900.

Learning of the possibility of selling these birds for such a sum, a fisherman caught one, but did not find a buyer so tore off its wings and threw the remains into the sea. A taxidermist recovered the pieces and reassembled them. Unfortunately his workshop and contents were destroyed a few months later. The last observation of the Guadalupe caracara was in December 1900.

A subspecies of Bewick's wren, *Thyromanes bewickii brevicaudus*, was discovered in 1875, the year when cats were introduced to the island and when a Dr Palmer collected two specimens. By 1887 the species was considered very rare, and in 1892 the last three known birds were killed in one day's hunt. Repeated searches have since then only served to confirm their extinction.

A subspecies of towhee, *Pipilo maculatus consobrinus*, was observed for the last time in 1897. It was the victim of rats, cats and hunting.

The South Pacific
The Islanders' Quarry

Cook was the great pioneer in this ocean too. The naturalists traveling with him on his voyages collected many species never found again.

New Zealand

New Zealand comprises two of the largest islands in the South Pacific. The fauna of this region is undoubtedly one of those most depleted by man.

Fish

The New Zealand grayling, *Prototroctes oxyrhynchus*, is an example of the comparatively few fish that have become extinct. Formerly an abundant and important food source for the Maori, its demise is believed to have been caused by destruction of its habitat, as the vegetation surrounding and overhanging rivers was cleared by settlers. The last specimens were caught in March 1923, in the North Island.

Birds

Although Macquarie Island is Australian territory, it is biologically part of New Zealand's outlying islands' ecosystem. Situated at latitude 55°S, it has a rigorous climate, with strong winds and sea spray restricting plant growth to lichens, mosses and a few grasses. Two endemic birds, a parrot and a rail, still lived there in 1880 when J.H. Scott of Otago University paid a visit. An 1894 expedition was unable to find any trace of them.

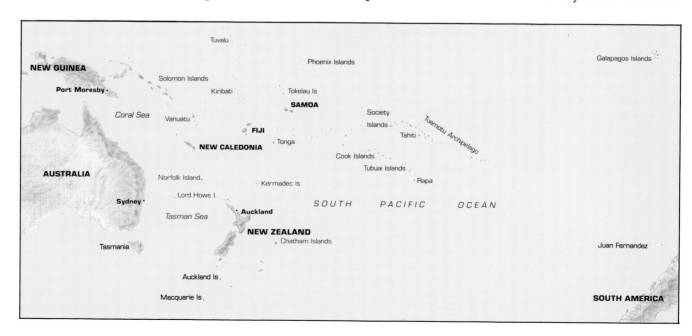

An endemic subspecies of parakeet, *Cyanoramphus novaezelandiae erythrotis*, was plentiful when the sealers and penguin hunters arrived. It had adapted to Macquarie's rigorous climate and made its nests under the tufts of grass. The introduction of cats was no doubt the main reason for its disappearance 74 years after the collection of the first specimens.

In 1879 a ship that had come to the island to hunt seals collected a live specimen of an endemic race of banded land rails, *Gallirallus philippensis*.

The New Zealand quail, *Coturnix novaezelandiae*, was collected for the first time during the voyage of the *Astrolabe*. Four specimens are preserved in the Natural History Museum in Paris. This quail was very plentiful during the colonization of the main islands at the beginning of the 19th century. However, their numbers decreased rapidly, no doubt as a result of overintensive hunting, burning grasslands, and the introduction of predators. The last reliable record is from 1875.

There were about 13 species of giant birds, the moas, some of which may still have been alive in remote areas until less than two centuries ago. The Maori, who came to New Zealand more than 1000 years ago, quickly learned to hunt the huge birds. The tallest moas grew to a little over 10 feet (3 meters) high, and could exceed 550 pounds (250 kilograms) in weight. The last authentic sightings may date from as recently as the 1800s, though many species, including the largest, were extinct much earlier.

Discovery of these birds by naturalists goes back to 1838, when a fragment of tibia was brought back to England and passed to the famous paleontologist Richard Owen. Some hunting accounts or descriptions of these gigantic birds were collected from Maori during the 1850s, and there have been many discoveries of bones left in piles among sand dunes by humans after a successful hunt.

The New Zealand quail, *Coturnix novaezelandiae*, was very plentiful during the colonization of the country in the early 19th century but the last reliable record of a sighting was filed in 1875.

There were probably 13 species of moas in New Zealand, the tallest being more than 10 feet (3 meters) tall. Last authentic sightings date as recently as the 1800s, though many species, including the largest, were extinct much earlier.

An owl, *Sceloglaux albifacies*, lived in New Zealand until the beginning of the 20th century. The North and South Islands each had a separate subspecies. In the Maori language, this owl was called *whekau*; in English, because its cry resembled a laugh, the bird was called the laughing owl. The last record dates from 1914.

The merganser, *Mergus australis*, endemic to the Auckland Islands, was discovered and described by Hombron and Jacquinot in 1840. Searches carried out by experienced ornithologists during the military occupation of the Auckland Islands in 1941–6 were all unsuccessful in rediscovering this bird; the last record dates from 1905.

The huia, *Heteralocha acutirostris*, had the most famous feathers of any New Zealand bird, standing for dignity and authority. The birds occurred only in the North Island, and their feathers were used in major ceremonies, and to adorn the cloaks of those who held high rank. This species showed strong differences between the male and the female in beak structure and length. Many observations, in particular those by Sir Walter Buller, have enabled us to understand them better. They fed on larvae and insects living in rotting tree trunks, the male's short, strong beak being able to take off the bark and seize the most accessible insects while the female could pull out the deeper larvae. During a visit to New Zealand, King George V received some huia feathers as a present. The passion for

The Auckland Island merganser, *Mergus australis*, discovered in 1840 during the voyage of the *Astrolabe*, had become extinct by 1905.

The huia, *Heterolocha acutirostris*, was prized for its feathers that signified dignity and authority in early Maori lore. The birds' skins and feathers were hunted with such intensity by white collectors at the end of last century that a rapid fall in numbers followed. The last sighting occurred in 1907.

collecting the birds' skins and their feathers was such that the huia, already rare, was hunted with irreversible effects at the end of last century. After a rapid fall in numbers, the last sighting occurred in 1907.

The Chatham Islands, east of mainland New Zealand, are famous for the masses of bones discovered there over the last 150 years, including bones of several species now extinct. The introduction of rats, cats and dogs added to the depredations of excessive hunting and the devastation caused by bush fires. The Chatham Island rail, *Cabalus modestus*, and Dieffenbach's rail, *Rallus philippensis dieffenbachi* (locally called *moeriki*) lived here. Both rails became extinct in the 19th century, in part because of hunting.

The modest rail, measuring a little less than 8 inches (20 centimeters), was discovered in 1871. Within 25 years it had disappeared from Mangere Island. Its survival on such a small island, with an area of less than half a square mile (1.3 square kilometers), has astonished many ornithologists. Earlier, it had been present on other islands of the Chathams group. Even more curious was the particular sexual dimorphism of this bird, a feature it shared with the extinct New Zealand huia; the beak of the male was much longer than that of the female. Twenty-six specimens have been listed around the world.

The endemic Chatham Island bellbird, *Anthornis melanura melanocephala*, was last observed on Mangere Island in 1906, and so died out early this century.

Exploits of the Lighthouse-keeper's Cat

The most notorious cat in this book must be the one owned by a lighthouse-keeper on Stephens Island, New Zealand, since it holds the record for the fastest-known extermination of a species. It is to this creature that we owe the 16 specimens preserved round the world of the Stephen Island wren, *Xenicus lyalli* — that it destroyed in just a year.

This extinction took place so swiftly that the British public learned of the existence of the bird and of its disappearance both at the same time. Upset by this news, the New Zealand public blamed the lighthouse-keepers, and suggested they should be forbidden to have cats as long as the state provided them with mousetraps. Deeply saddened by the extinction of the wren, ornithologists did, however, recognize that the cat had been generous in not eating the little birds on the spot, thus enabling them to have specimens of it.

New Caledonia

The first human settlements on this large island, 3000 years ago or more, destroyed most of its large animals. Cultivation of the coastal plains is thought to have profoundly modified the fauna and flora, causing the extinction of smaller species such as *Leucocharis*, a snail a few millimeters long, just one specimen of which was collected about 1860.

Birds

The megapodes are a family of Galliformes distinguished principally by the fact that they do not sit on their eggs to hatch them, but lay them in a plant mass they have previously built up, so that its decomposition will provide the necessary heat. The 'nests' of the Australian megapodes can reach a height of 20 feet (6 meters) and a diameter of 35 feet (10.7 meters). The chick is very precocious and, barely hatched, is able to fly.

The New Caledonian megapode, *Megapodius molestructor*, is known from fossil bones contemporary with man. William Anderson was the surgeon's mate on board the *Resolution* during Cook's second voyage, during which he made his only call at New Caledonia. Although he had been given no responsibilities as a naturalist, he mentioned a bird he called *Tetrao australis*. However, since he described it as having bare legs, and since all grouse (*Tetrao*) have their legs feathered right down to the toes, this bird might well have been a megapode.

The presence in New Caledonia of mounds of unknown origin has caused a lot of speculation; some think they are man-made, while others see them as giant birds' nests. In fact they contain no more vegetable matter than pieces of shell, and today the only acceptable explanation of the origin of these structures is the archeological one.

Sylviornis neocaledoniae was a giant galliforme, measuring more than 4 feet (1.3 meters) from head to tail. Seventeen hundred years ago, this strange bird was the most plentiful in the group. It is thought to have disappeared before the arrival of the Europeans.

The New Caledonian owlet nightjar, *Aegotheles savesi*, is the largest of the whole family of Aegothelidae that is endemic to the region from Halamahera through New Guinea and Australia to New Caledonia. Only

The New Caledonian megapode was discovered during Cook's second voyage, as proved by the description by William Anderson, surgeon's mate on board the *Resolution*.

The New Caledonian owlet-nightjar, *Aegotheles savesi* (left). The sole specimen was caught in a bedroom of a private house near Noumea in 1880.

one specimen is known, in the Merseyside County Museum, at Liverpool. It was captured in 1880, in a bedroom at Tonghoué, near Noumea. Some 20 years ago a hunter claimed to have seen one in the Paita area, and to have shot it while it was asleep on a branch. Since then, bones have been found in caves.

Further research should make it possible to confirm the survival of some of these species, particularly the nocturnal birds of prey.

The kagu, which is the emblem of New Caledonia and top priority on the world list of endangered birds, has a close relationship with the extinct species, *Rhynochetus aurarius*, whose remains have been discovered in caves. Larger than the present-day kagu, it no doubt frequented the coastal areas and was thus under earlier threat. Today, about a thousand kagus survive in secluded areas of the mountains.

The extinct diurnal birds of prey include two species of goshawks, *Accipiter efficax* and *Accipiter quartus*, both of which disappeared before the arrival of the European explorers. The first of these was powerful; the second was particularly small. Their disappearance no doubt followed closely on the extinction of the species they preyed on.

Lafresnaye's rail, *Tricholimnas lafresnayanus*, was endemic. Some 20 specimens have been preserved. It had an olive-brown plumage, and was once plentiful in the Noumea area; most of the specimens came from the swamps of Dumbea and Saint-Louis. Although none has been collected in more than 50 years, these birds no doubt survive in the northeast of the island, as many reports suggest, and indeed the author may have seen one in November 1984.

Another rail, *Porphyrio kukwiedei*, a giant swamp-hen measuring 30 inches (76 centimeters) from beak to tail, is thought to have disappeared about a century ago, having been hunted on the west coast with snares by the Kanaks at the time of the 1878 insurrection.

This giant of New Caledonia, *Sylviornis neocaledoniae*, was a peaceful vegetarian that 1700 years ago appeared to be the most plentiful bird in the group. It is thought to have disappeared before the arrival of Europeans.

The lorikeet *Charmosyna diadema* is known only by two specimens. The first, that serves as type for the species, was shown to the public at the French Permanent Exhibition of Products from Algeria and the Colonies in 1860. The second was captured in 1911 or 1912, but arrived in such a decomposed state that it was thrown away. One observation of this species was made in 1986, in a forested area of the mountains, so this lorikeet, measuring just under 8 inches (20 centimeters), may still survive.

The emblem of New Caledonia, the kagu, is the cousin of this extinct *Rhynochetus aurarius*. The latter was larger than today's species and was a shore dweller whose bones have frequently been found in caves.

The New Caledonian buttonquail, *Turnix neocaledoniae*, long assimilated into the Australian species (*T. varia*) that was introduced there several times, was in fact an endemic species, present before human settlement, as bones have been found in cave levels below the first traces of human remains. Only a few stuffed specimens are known. By some accounts, it is possible a quail has survived on an almost deserted islet. Is it the endemic or the introduced one?

A grass owl, *Tyto letocarti*, slightly larger than the barn owl, though not related to it, disappeared not long after the arrival of humans and rats.

A snipe, probably belonging to a native species of the genus *Coenochorypha*, has been found in a west coast cave. Unfortunately it is known so far only by a fragment of humerus, and its relationships are still difficult to determine.

Two pigeons — a ground dove, *Gallicolumba longitarsus*, and *Caloenas canacorum*, a species close to the Nicobar pigeon — have become extinct in no doubt very similar conditions.

Caloenas canacorum, a close relative of the Nicobar pigeon, inhabited the New Caledonian mainland.

Reptiles

The present reptile fauna of New Caledonia includes 50 species of geckos and small lizards. The largest species have become very rare today, but research has revealed the extinction of three very large species.

An as yet unnamed fossil monitor lizard, closely related to a New Guinea species but probably endemic, was discovered in 1983. Lizards are the subject of many legends, and are furthermore often considered as ancestors by mountain tribes. During my research in these areas, several sincere persons stated they had seen the monitor on the northeast coast. One hunter even claimed to have killed one, 20 years ago, near Boulouparis on the western side, and said he had preserved its jaw for about 10 years.

The crocodile *Mekosuchus inexpectatus*, measuring more than 6½ feet (2 meters), lived on chickens, giant birds, and other reptiles. It was unusual in having a purely terrestrial habitat, and it has many other features recalling the extinct crocodiles of the Mesozoic. Its origins go back more than 90 million years. Its disappearance seems to be due to man, since a skull fragment has been found at the bottom of a kitchen midden.

The crocodile *Mekosuchus inexpectatus* was a very primitive terrestrial form, many of its features being reminiscent of Mesozoic species.

The tortoise *Meiolania* lived on the main island and on Tiga and Walpole. It had horns on its head, protecting plates on its feet and tail, and its shell could be as long as 4 feet (1.3 meters). Its rapid extermination resulted no doubt from it being eaten. Biologists have difficulty in understanding how such large tortoises could survive on such small islets and how, since they could not swim, they managed to settle on them.

The extinct tortoise *Meiolania* lived on the New Caledonian mainland and the islets of Tiga and Walpole in the Loyalty group. Its shell could be as long as 4 feet (1.3 meters). It was also once present in Australia and on Lord Howe Island.

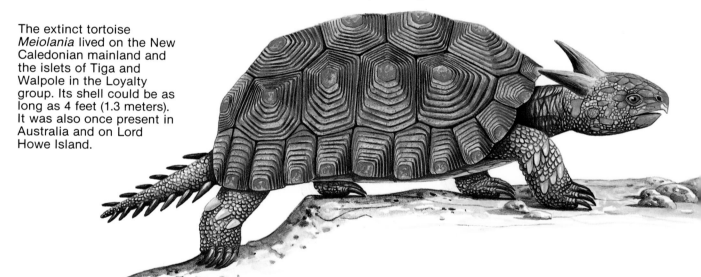

Banks, Tonga, Kermadecs, Samoa, Wallis

Historical data suggest that several species of megapodes once inhabited various islands of the central South Pacific. One lived on Tikopia in the Banks group. Eggs were collected last century on Hapai Island in the Tongan group, while traditions on the island of Levuka mention the earlier existence of another megapode. Various accounts relating to the Kermadecs mention yet another, but their authenticity is not completely proved. Last century eggs that were also attributed to megapodes were gathered in Samoa, but the birds that laid them have never been identified. On Savai'i, in Samoa, there was a small nocturnal gallinule, *Pareudiastes pacificus*, last captured in 1873.

On the island of Tongatapu, the largest of the Tongan group, there was until 1800 an endemic subspecies of flycatcher, *Pomarea nigra tabuensis*, that Forster had described during Cook's second voyage, on the basis of one specimen, a female.

Wallis Island, nearly 250 miles (400 kilometers) northeast of Fiji, is only 9 miles (14 kilometers) long. Archeological deposits brought to light by French research work over the last 4 years have yielded the remains of an extinct species of Imperial pigeon, *Ducula david*, that is the largest of all the known species of this genus. The Tongans, and no doubt many other Polynesians, had an immoderate love of hunting pigeons. It was a sport reserved for the nobility, and rather like a clay pigeon shoot; the nobles killed birds deliberately released near promontories on which the hunters were installed. The only known specimens are about 2500 years old.

An extinct Imperial pigeon, *Ducula david*, the largest of its genus, used to live on Wallis Island. The only known specimens are about 2500 years old. Many Polynesians, and particularly the Tongans, had an immoderate love of pigeon hunting, a sport often reserved for royalty.

Lord Howe

Lord Howe Island, east of Australia, has an area of only 5½ square miles (14 square kilometers). It was once inhabited by many bird species.

White-throated pigeons of the subspecies *Columba vitiensis godmanae* were very plentiful and not afraid of man. Ships' crews had no difficulty in catching them on branches because they did not fly away. Once they were captured their legs were broken, and the cries of suffering from these unfortunate birds then attracted all the others in the neighborhood, so that they too were then taken. They are thought to have become extinct in 1853.

An endemic subspecies of the red-fronted parrot, *Cyanoramphus novaezelandiae subflavescens*, was plentiful at the time of the island's discovery, but considered harmful by farmers because the parrots ate seeds

On Lord Howe Island there
was a giant swamp hen,
Porphyrio albus, with white
plumage sometimes
marked with blue.
Scientists interpret this as
a case of insular albinism.

and destroyed seedlings. The last parrots observed, a pair, were seen in 1869.

A giant white rail, *Porphyrio albus*, rivalling the New Zealand takahe for size, was also hunted. The color of these birds varied considerably from all white or all blue, to blue and white. This coloring seems to have resulted from albinism, frequent among other island species.

Norfolk

Norfolk Island, halfway between New Zealand and New Caledonia, used to have a rich fauna of birds. The parrot *Nestor productus*, related to the New Zealand kaka, lived in the forests here and on Phillip Island, which was its last refuge. It lived on the nectar of flowers such as the hibiscus. In 1841 John Gould wrote that man had made such inroads on its original habitat, and brought it so close to extinction that the day was not far off when, like the dodo, it would be known only from its skin and bones.

In fact even paleontological research has been able to discover only a few rare bones of this parrot. The last specimen died in a cage in London in 1851. Gould described the species from the specimen held in Sydney by a Major Anderson. The bird seemed to have adapted to human com-

The parrot *Nestor
productus*, although easily
tamed, disappeared from
Norfolk Island with the
destruction of its habitat in
1851. The last specimen
died in captivity.

The Norfolk Island pigeon, *Hemiphaga novæzelandiae spadicea*, disappeared in 1801 because of intensive hunting.

pany, ate lettuce, and liked fruit juice, cream and butter. Gould, fascinated by this specimen, concluded that the parrot stood up well to captivity, was easily satisfied, of good disposition, and a pleasant companion.

Fiji

Fiji's original environment is in constant regression, and naturalists have only been able to study a fraction of the species that have lived on these islands. Furthermore, a number of species have acclimatized so well that they compete strongly with the native ones.

Other species have been extinct for centuries, as recent fossil discoveries suggest. Archeological digs in the Lau group have revealed the existence of giant megapodes that were contemporary with the first inhabitants but have today vanished. Recent surveys by the author brought to light in 1986 the first fossil-bearing sites on Viti Levu.

In historical times, *Nesoclopeus poeciloptera*, a large rail nearly 2 feet (60 centimeters) long, lived on Ovalau and Viti Levu. It frequented marshy areas and seems to have been totally flightless. Its disappearance cannot be definitely recorded because of recent possible (though unconfirmed) sightings. Its rarity seems to have resulted as much from the destruction of its habitat as from the depredations of introduced rats and mongooses.

Solomon Islands and Vanuatu

The Solomon Islands and Vanuatu (formerly the New Hebrides) are obscure areas for naturalists, and research is difficult there, the reasons being in part political. Some species are, however, known to have disappeared from these groups.

Tanna, one of the islands of Vanuatu, was disovered by Cook in 1774. The island is volcanic and in the forest the naturalist Forster discovered a dove, *Gallicolumba ferruginea*. The only known specimen is the one he killed on August 17, 1774, and of which his son did a drawing. He described it as a small bird with rust-brown head and breast, and distinguished from the other new pigeons they discovered by its dark-green wings and strange yellow eyes. It seems that it lived on nuts, and in particular on a kind of nutmeg peculiar to the island.

Meek's pigeon, *Microgoura meeki*, of Choiseul in the Solomon Islands, is known only from six specimens collected in 1904. These were no doubt

The Choiseul pigeon, *Microgoura meeki*, is known only from the specimens obtained during a traditional ceremony in the Solomons in 1904.

The dove *Gallicolumba ferruginea* was discovered on Tanna in Vanuatu by J.R. Forster. The bird he killed in August 1774 is the only known specimen.

obtained during a traditional ceremony. No subsequent searches have been able to locate this pigeon. Hunted by the islanders for its flesh, it was also preyed on by cats. Members of the Whitney South Sea Expedition in 1927 and 1929 could not find this superb bird. In 1904 the islanders mentioned that the species was becoming rare, that they had seen none for many years, and said that cats were responsible for their extermination.

Juan Fernandez

Sandalwood, *Santalum fernandezianum*, from Robinson Crusoe Island, disappeared early in the 20th century. This semi-parasitic plant, with red fruits, was the object of frenzied gathering that is believed to have resulted in its extinction in 1916, although some searchers still hope to rediscover it.

Galapagos Islands

The Galapagos Islands, lying in the Pacific Ocean east of Ecuador, are one of the the world's most famous nature reserves. Their unique fauna, closely studied by the famous naturalist Charles Darwin, includes a remarkably diverse group of at least 14 subspecies of the tortoise *Geochelone elephantopus*, each endemic to a particular island of the group. Known to seafarers as 'Galapagos mutton', they were first plundered in the 17th century, and within 300 years four of these subspecies have become extinct. This was an ironic fate for the creatures that played a significant part in Darwin's development of the theory of 'survival of the fittest.'

French Polynesia

Rapa

The forest of Rapa used to be home to about 100 species of land snails. None has survived the total destruction of the vegetation.

Tahiti

Tahiti used to have a sandpiper, *Prosobonia leucoptera*, only three specimens of which are now known. Its name was *torote* or *te te*. It frequented the banks of watercourses. This habitat was quickly invaded, and pigs, dogs and cats destroyed the young in their nests. It does not seem that this bird lasted beyond Cook's visit. A neighboring species, *Prosobonia ellisi*, was on Moorea, but is now only known from a painting. Today it is considered possible that these two are in fact the same species.

The Tahitian sandpiper, *Prosobonia leucoptera*, is known only from three specimens. Pigs, cats, and rats exterminated it in just a few years.

In 1773 Cook also discovered on Tahiti and Ra'iatea a black-fronted parrot, *Cyanoramphus zealandicus*, two specimens of which he took back to London. In 1844 a further example was taken to France by Lieutenant de Marolles. On Ra'iatea the bird's name was *aa*. The species is thought to have disappeared in the 1850s.

The Tahiti rail, *Gallirallus ecaudata*, is known only by the painting done of it by Forster, one of the naturalists travelling with Cook. The Polynesian name of this bird was *tevea*. Only a femur discovered during an archeological dig in a marae of the Papenoo Valley is considered to validate the existence of this species, but it cannot be definitive since we have no other specimen to compare it with.

The Samoan rail, *Pareudiastes pacificus*,
was captured for the last time in 1873.

The starling *Aplonis mavornata* is something of a mystery, known only from one specimen. Its preservation was so poor that it was very difficult to determine the characteristics of the species, and its existence was for a long time a matter of controversy. No other observation enables us to fix the geographical origin of this species that has since become extinct. Its discoverer, surgeon-naturalist William Anderson, died of consumption before his collections got back to England, leaving no precise indication that might enable a better identification of the species. Moreover, this specimen was nearly 100 years old when the biologist Sharpe studied it, and it had deteriorated badly from poor preservation, resembling a dusty mummy that had faded in the sun. Some wondered whether it was the Ra'iatea thrush collected by Cook. Streseman's study of 1949 seems to have closed the debate and confirmed that the specimen belongs to the genus *Aplonis*.

A thrush was collected on Ra'iatea by Cook's crew, in May 1774. Its name was recorded as *eboonae-bou-nou*. This strange bird, the sole specimen of which is today lost, was drawn by George Forster and described by Latham. The specimen was placed in the collection of Sir Joseph Banks, another member of the expedition, but had disappeared by the time the collection reached the British Museum. The species must have already been very rare because its habitat seems to have been restricted to the steep valleys.

A thrush, *Turdus ulietensis*, was collected on Ra'iatea in the last week of May 1774. Forster's description of it is so precise that it is clearly a different species from the one discussed above.

The Atlantic Ocean
The Island Fox and the Volcano Rat

The 41 million square miles (105 million square kilometers) of the Atlantic are virtually unbroken except for a few hundred islands, which vary greatly in size. Christopher Columbus was the first to cross the Atlantic in 1492.

The West Indies, also known as the Antilles, form the biggest archipelago in the Atlantic, and are among the most densely populated islands in the

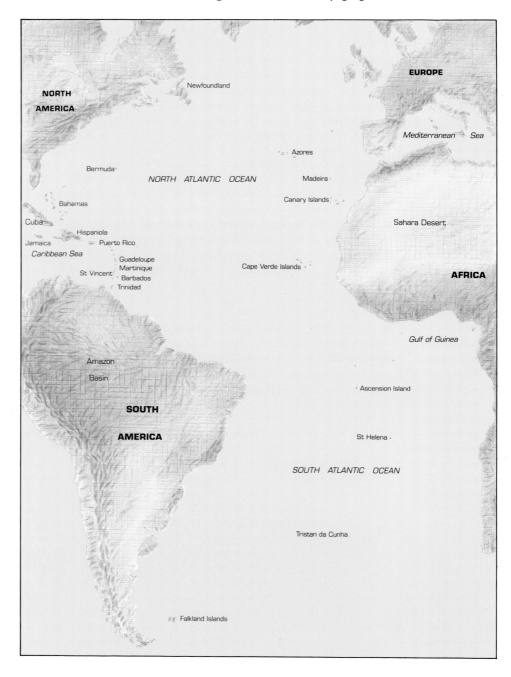

world. This overpopulation has resulted in the destruction of almost all the forests and the extinction of more than 40 species of birds and mammals.

Furthermore, several human groups have been exterminated by the Europeans; in the Antilles, for example, the Arawak Indians, whose ancient culture may go back to 2500 B.C. In the process of colonization, the native peoples, then numbering more than half a million, were exterminated. Black slaves suffered from poverty and disease. Later, freebooters and buccaneers made themselves notorious by their misdeeds.

The present-day fauna includes more than 100 species near extinction. About 10 of these were long considered to have disappeared, but have recently been rediscovered. They include the petrel *Pterodroma cahow*, which was first rediscovered in the early 20th century when just four specimens were found. Later, in 1951, colonies of about 100 birds were discovered on neighboring islets, so the species is now considered to be making a slow recovery. Certain West Indian insectivores — the Haitian solenodon *Solenodon paradoxus*, the Cuban solenodon or almiqui, *Atopogale cubana,* and the Hispaniolan hytia, *Plagiodontia aedium* — were long regarded as extinct, but were found again in north-east Hispaniola, eastern Cuba and Haiti.

Marine Fauna

The West Indian monk seal, *Monachus tropicalis*, is today the only species of seal destroyed by man. It used to come ashore in this region to breed.

A representation of the discovery of the West Indies by Christopher Columbus.

The West Indian monk seal, *Monachus tropicalis* became extinct in about 1954. It is so far the only species of seal destroyed by man.

The hunt for its fur and meat brought about rapid extinction in the mid-20th century.

The great auk, *Pinguinis impennis*, measured up to about 2 feet (60 centimeters) and was flightless, with only vestigial wings. (Wing reduction occurs with other contemporary members of the family Alcidae, adapting them remarkably for swimming, without limiting their flying capacity, although they do need long distances to take off.) Distribution of this species was once extremely wide, as is shown by the fossil bones discovered in North America and Greenland, in Scotland and Scandinavia, and even down to France and Italy. Human consumption of the bird is proved by the innumerable bones found in middens.

The earliest known mention of the species is by the explorer Jacques Cartier in 1538. In 1590 an Icelander filled a whole ship with the skins of this bird. A colony on Funk Island, off Newfoundland, which no doubt was the largest ever found in one locality, was exterminated in just a few years, and when the Norwegian, Stuwitz, landed there in 1841, all that was left was piles of bones, a few mummified specimens, and egg debris. Sailors often used the auks as fish bait. Several tens of millions of these birds are thought to have been destroyed for their meat, feathers or fat. The last specimen was killed on Eldez Island, off Iceland, in 1844. Ninety skins have been preserved; their dates of capture are only rarely recorded, but it is notable that those for which we do have dates were mostly killed in spring, while nesting.

Egg collectors are the creators of an unbelievable market in fossil auk eggs, that are valued at up to 30 times their weight in gold.

The West Indies

As in most tropical islands, a rich fauna, particularly of birds, had developed here. The main causes of their extinctions were hunting and the introduction of new mammals — accidentally, as with the rat, or deliberately, as with the mongoose, which was introduced in 1870 to control poisonous

The great auk, *Pinguinis impennis*. Distribution of this species was once extremely wide but several tens of millions of the birds are thought to have been destroyed for their meat, feathers or fat. The last specimens disappeared in 1844.

ANIMALES PREHISTORICOS **7**

Aquila borrasi

CUBA CORREOS 1982

The Cuban eagle, *Aquila borrasi*, is known only from fossil bones.

The nightjar, *Siphonornis americanus*, endemic to Jamaica; the last specimens were a pair captured in 1850.

snakes, in particular the notoriously lethal pit viper. However, the imprecise accounts and the absence of ophidian specimens earlier than this introduction mean the reasons for extinction of some of these snakes are inconclusive. On the other hand, the mongooses and the rats, dogs and cats, as well as abusive hunting, are certainly responsible for the disappearance of more than a score of notable species.

Birds

Siphonornis americanus, a nightjar endemic to Jamaica, is now known only by a very few stuffed or preserved specimens. The last individuals are thought to have been a pair captured in 1850. Although many attempts to rediscover this species were subsequently organized, none was successful. The extinction resulted from hunting by humans and the depredations of introduced predators, especially cats.

The West Indian birds of prey have suffered heavily from deforestation, and especially from the disappearance of the big mammals and rodents. In Cuba, for example, an eagle, *Aquila borrasi*, a vulture, and three species of owls became extinct. The largest of these, *Ornimegalonyx*, must have been more than 3½ feet (1.1 meters) long. The disappearance of these

One of the three extinct parrots of Guadeloupe, *Anadorhynchus purpurescens*, had plumage of a uniform blue-purple.

birds no doubt followed that of the big mammals that were their prey, of which only a few bones remain. Two subspecies of the burrowing owl, *Speotyto cunicularia amaura* and *S.c. guadeloupensis*, disappeared at the end of the 19th century, not long after the introduction of mongooses and rats. The Guadeloupe subspecies was nicknamed the *coucou-terre* or ground cuckoo, because of its song. There remain only 11 specimens of these two subspecies.

Another group suffering greatly from the presence of humans is the parrots. The Arawak Indians apparently had already hunted them intensively, and several species had probably already disappeared before the Europeans arrived. An example is the Sainte Croix macaw, *Ara autochtones*, that is known only from a tibia found in a midden by archeologists.

The Cuban macaw, *Ara tricolor*, is known only from five specimens, one of which was kept in the Ménagerie in Paris, where it died in 1842. This species lived on Cuba and the Isle of Pines and measured about 20 inches (50 centimeters). The last known individual was killed in 1864 during a game hunt near the Vega. Extinction of this species seems to have been caused by both hunting and deforestation.

The Jamaican yellow-headed macaw, *Ara gossei*, is known from a single specimen that today is lost. It was killed in 1765 by a Mr. Odell, while hunting east of Lucea.

The green and yellow macaw, *Ara erythrocephala*, also of Jamaica, is unfortunately known only from a description, and indeed its very existence is a matter of some doubt. The only description we have is dated 1842 and refers to a green and yellow parrot. In the same year a Rev. Mr. Loward may have observed two more at the foot of the mountains in St. John Parish; these may have been the last representatives of the species.

The parrot *Ara erythrura* is known only from two accounts.

The Jamaican yellow-headed macaw, *Ara gossei*, is known from a single specimen that was killed in 1765 and subsequently lost.

The Dominican macaw, *Ara atwoodi*, disappeared in the 1800s, again the victim of hunting.

A subspecies of the Hispaniolan conure, *Aratinga chloroptera maugei*, that lived on Mona Island and perhaps Puerto Rico, disappeared in 1892 and only three specimens of it are known. The last living bird was no doubt the one now in the Natural History Museum in Paris; it appears to have died in the Ménagerie. The other subspecies is still common in the mountains of Hispaniola.

The orange-bellied macaw of Martinique, *Anodorhynchus martinicus*, was described in 1635 as being twice or three times the size of the parrots and having a very differently colored plumage of blue and orange feathers.

Four other species of parrot have apparently also disappeared, but no specimen survives. The old descriptions that remain are, however, sufficiently detailed to recognize the birds as an authentic though extinct species.

The violet macaw, *Anodorhynchus purpurescens*, had uniformly bluish plumage. It lived on Guadeloupe, where it was called *oné couli*. A violet parrot, *Amazona violacea*, described in 1788, lived on Guadeloupe, and another species, *Amazona martinica*, described in 1905, lived on Martinique.

Also on Guadeloupe was another parrot, *Conurus labati*, with a white beak and totally green plumage except for a few red feathers on the head. The writer Labat described the bird as amiable, affectionate and easily taught to speak, but it became extinct in about 1722.

On Dominica, halfway between Guadeloupe and Martinique, there was a petrel, *Aestrelata caribbaea*. Discovered in 1866, it became extinct in the 1930s.

> It is a nocturnal bird living in burrows . . . The burrow or tunnel is 6–10 feet (2–3 meters) long and ends in a space large enough to lodge the pair. They leave it at night, flying off to seek food (fish)

The Caribbean petrel, *Aestrelata caribbæa*, was still common on Dominica in 1906 but had become extinct by the 1930s.

. . . They are often seen by moonlight or at sunrise near their nests and sometimes crossing the road, with no concern for workers going off to their jobs. (Du Tertre.)

In 1906 it was still common, as B.H. Verril makes clear:

At nightfall one can often see them flying near the cliffs along with myriads of bats that spend their days in the cracks and fissures. It is difficult to procure any, and although they are quite often shot at, only two specimens have been obtained.

A subspecies of the reddish-brown uniform rail, endemic to Jamaica, *Aramides concolor concolor*, was collected for the last time in 1881, a victim of rats, cats, and mongooses as well as hunters.

A subspecies of the house wren, indigenous to Martinique, *Troglodytes aedon martinicensis*, has not been seen since 1886, despite the many ornithological expeditions to this island. It may have been made extinct by mongooses, cats, rats, or possibly the boa constrictor.

A subspecies of bullfinch, *Loxigila portoricensis grandis*, was living on Puerto Rico until the introduction of African monkeys that ate the eggs from their nests and so caused their extinction about 1900.

The Martinque muskrat or pilori, *Megalomys demarestii*, used to hide its head in the ground when it scented danger. First discovered in 1654, the species' last representatives were destroyed by a mountain eruption in 1902.

Mammals

West Indian mammals include a dozen extinct species, some dating from the first human settlement more than 2000 years ago; and others, more numerous, following the introduction of predators, the clearing of forests, and the cultivation of land. Three rodents, a bat, and an insectivore are among the main recent victims.

Until very recently, several species of rodent existed, including *Megalomys demarestii* and *M. luciae*. The Martinique muskrat or pilori (*Megalomys demarestii*) was first described in 1654 in Du Tertre's *Histoire Générale des Îsles de Saint-Christophe, de la Guadeloupe, de la Martinique et autre Îles dans l'Amérique*. This author mentions the regular hunting of it by the island's inhabitants, who 'were not repelled by the musky smell of its flesh.' Some early accounts comment on the quite original behavior of this rodent, which hid its head like an ostrich when it scented danger. It was reputed to harm crops. Its extinction was advanced enough for only a few remaining groups to find refuge on the slopes of Mt. Pelée, which in all likelihood destroyed the last representatives during its eruption in 1902. Only six specimens are known, and searches undertaken since the eruption have proved fruitless.

The other closely related rodent, *M. luciae*, distinguished by a more brownish belly, only the throat being white, lived on St. Lucia. Two specimens are known; one of them was placed in the Ménagerie of the Jardin des Plantes in Paris in August 1851, and died there later the same year.

The isolobodons (hutia) of the Dominican Republic and Puerto Rico, rodents about the size of rabbits, were much appreciated for their meat. Archeological discoveries even suggest that these animals were raised in semi-captivity. The Haitian species, *Isolobodon levir*, was to disappear before European contact, and the Puerto Rican species, *I. portoricensis*, about 1700.

Two species of rice rats, *Oryzomys antillarum* on Jamaica and *O. victus* on St. Vincent, were to disappear in 1877 and 1897, respectively. Their extinctions seem attributable to the introduced mongooses.

Some large edentate mammals survived for some time after the arrival of the first human settlers. These animals, for example the Cuban ground sloth *Megalocnus*, could reach the height of a black bear. The remains of two other genera of sloth, *Acratocnus* and *Parocnus*, were found in association with human remains, thus proving that humans and these species once existed at the same time.

The Cuban shrew or solenodon, *Solenodon cubanus*, was not well known to naturalists until the 1850s. This strange mammal, the size of a cat, may be related to other Malagasy and African insectivores. From 1866 on, naturalists had great difficulty in gathering a few specimens. The last one disappeared in 1910. The Burman mongoose, introduced about 1870, seems to have been one of the main agents of extermination.

The Greater Antilles fruit-eating bat, *Sternoderma rufum*, is known only from the single specimen in the Natural History Museum in Paris. Isidore Geoffroy Saint-Hilaire described it in 1812 when he was still unaware of where it came from. It was only from other bones of this species, discovered in Puerto Rico in 1918, that the source was determined. The bats in this part of the world are particularly abundant and are essentially fruit-eaters. It appears the reason they became extinct was the destruction of the trees whose fruit was their main food.

Several species of vampire bat also inhabited the main West Indian islands, but rapidly disappeared when the large mammals whose blood they sucked were exterminated by humans.

Megalocnus, the Cuban ground sloth, was a large edentate mammal as tall as a black bear.

Falklands

The Falklands fox, *Dusicyon australis*, was endemic to the Falkland Islands. It was twice as big as the European fox and as large as an English mastiff. It was the only predator known on the group, and also the islands' largest terrestrial vertebrate. It was discovered in 1689–90, and one animal was embarked on the *Welfare*. After the fox had been in the hold for several months, the ship became involved in a battle with the French fleet, during which the fox jumped overboard.

The animal's reputation rapidly crossed the Atlantic. Castaway sailors from various ships, and Bougainville's crews, had been attacked by hordes of this aggressive quadruped. In 1764 Lord Byron even reported that to get rid of the creatures the crew had set fire to the grass, so that 'they will be routed from this part of the Country, as it has been in a blaze as far as one can see for these three days past.' The fur trade, and the need to protect domestic animals from the fox, hastened its extinction, and hundreds of pelts were still being sold in 1840. One live specimen reached London in 1868. It was put in the zoo where it survived for a few years.

During his voyage on the *Beagle*, Charles Darwin, the famous naturalist, was to note the existence of this fox, three specimens of which he collected. The father of evolution posed many questions about the origins of this animal, of which he could find no close relative. He also remarked:

> I think, be doubted, that as the islands are now being colonised, before the paper is decayed on which this animal has been figured,

The Falklands fox, *Dusicyon australis*, was to disappear 20 years after Darwin had forecast its future extinction.

Mammalia Pl. 1

it will be ranked among those species that have perished from the Earth.

Because the inhabitants of these isolated islands accused the fox of vampirism, hunting of it was intensified, and the last Falklands fox disappeared in 1876, 17 years after the date of publication of Darwin's famous *On the Origin of Species*. He had been right again.

The king penguin, still plentiful in many places, also lived on the Falklands. It disappeared at the hands of animal traders and fishermen who cooked up the birds to extract the fat for caulking their ships and houses.

Canary Islands

The Canary Islands, situated off the West African coast, today have only a very impoverished fauna.

Naturalists have visited them frequently, and have drawn up a list of extinct species, even though, since then, further disappearances by human agency have occurred. The most recent of these, that happened while this work was being written, concerned a newly described species of puffin, formerly very plentiful on Fuerteventura Island. It had been discovered in the same year (1984) by three independent teams of Spanish, British, and French researchers.

An extinct finch has also been recently described.

Among the indigenous mammals, the large rodent, *Canariomys*, is now known only by one present-day species; another species of this endemic genus,

A rare species of lotus from the Canary Islands, *Lotus berthelotii*, is now extinct in Nature, but still survives in cultivation.

found in cave deposits contemporary with humans, is in the process of being described.

The plants of the Canary Islands have also suffered from deforestation, and some 10 species are said to have as good as disappeared. An example is the legume *Lotus berthelotii*, considered very rare at its discovery in 1895, then accepted to be almost certainly extinct. Today it survives essentially because it is cultivated. Also the tree *Trochetia erythroxylon* is almost extinct; only one sterile specimen is still alive.

Saint Helena, Cape Verde, Tristan da Cunha

St. Helena, a small island of 47 square miles (122 square kilometers), became famous in 1815 when Napoleon landed there in exile that was to end with his death six years later.

The island was discovered on May 21, 1502, by the Portuguese admiral, Joao da Nova Castella. It was then uninhabited. Goats were introduced in 1513, along with ducks, geese, and hens. Unfortunately, the goats became feral, causing a great deal of damage. Cats and dogs quickly multiplied, to the point where they had to be hunted from 1634 on.

It is claimed that a blue pigeon endemic to St. Helena disappeared about 1775. However, no written records have been found to prove its past existence or even to give it a name.

The flora and fauna of St. Helena were not studied by naturalists until long after the introduction of rats and various livestock. The most

The St. Helena hoopoe is known only from fossil bones.

astonishing thing is the total absence of any description of even a single endemic species. All attention was directed towards the introduced species, and so it is not surprising that no account has been found of the extinct birds of the island. Despite this, the list is extensive; a hoopoe, an endemic genus of cuckoo and another of pigeon, two species of rail, and two extinct members of the petrel and shearwater family (Procellariidae).

Several species of plants were destroyed, the most famous being no doubt the ebony tree, *Melhania melanoxylon*, used as fuel to produce lime. The great forests of the island were entirely felled by the beginning of the 19th century. With the destruction of the forest cover, several species of land snail, Helenoconcha in particular, were annihilated.

The Cape Verde Islands also had a giant lizard, *Macroscincus coctaei*. Its disappearance is said to go back to the 1940s, and searches in 1979 revealed none. This big skink was essentially vegetarian in diet, but occasionally ate petrel eggs and chicks. It was regularly hunted by the fishermen and other inhabitants of the islands. It was the largest member of this family of lizard; the biggest specimen measured 24 inches (62 cm). It lived on Ilheo Branco Island, and appears to have been hunted to extinction. One report records that in 1833, during a terrible famine, 'the island authorities ordered the transportation to Ilheo Branco of some thirty scoundrels who stayed there until the famine was over, living on plenty of fish and lizards. These men were able to profit by the episode and the lizards' fat is still used as an embrocation on painful spots.'

Tristan da Cunha, lost in the midst of the South Atlantic, had until 1890 an endemic moorhen, the Tristan gallinule, *Gallinula nesiotis*. Jonathan Lambert, who lived there, wrote in 1811 that there was a large number of them, that their flesh was delicate, and that in the preceding year he had caught about a hundred with a dog. In 1882, with the wreck of the *Henry B. Paul*, rats arrived and the species disappeared in less than ten years.

One of the six known specimens of *Macroscincus coctaei*, a giant lizard from the Cape Verde Islands, was photographed alive in 1873. The species disappeared in the 1940s.

The Mediterranean
A Reservoir of Pygmy Animals

The present fauna of the Mediterranean islands is rich in introduced species but ominously poor in endemic ones. Mammals and birds alike, the endemic species have been exterminated by humans, sometimes centuries ago. As with all island environments, the biggest and most desirable species disappeared first as a result of excessive hunting.

Apart from a dwarf 'goat' native to the Balearic Islands, there seems to have been no effort made to domesticate the various species that were endemic to each of the Mediterranean islands. On the other hand, many other species, European or African in origin, have been introduced.

The human species settled the islands long ago, dating from the upper Paleolithic and the Holocene. About 9000 years ago, in Sardinia, there was a variety of pygmies that possessed many primitive characteristics and was further distinguished from modern humans by having both small incisors and large molars.

These islands demonstrate the destructive power of primitive people who in less than 10,000 years, and without the introduction of any particularly devastating predators, still managed to bring about the disappearance of 30 species of large vertebrates.

The fauna of these islands has never been as diverse as on tropical islands, and now there are only a few endemic species left.

The main islands — Corsica and Sardinia, Sicily, the Balearics, Crete, Cyprus, the Cyclades — witnessed the evolution of a new fauna with European and African affinities. The island environment brought into being new, endemic forms that, in the case of the biggest species such as the elephants, hippopotamuses, and deer, usually became dwarf forms. Most of them also had shortened limbs, although it is not understood why or how this came about.

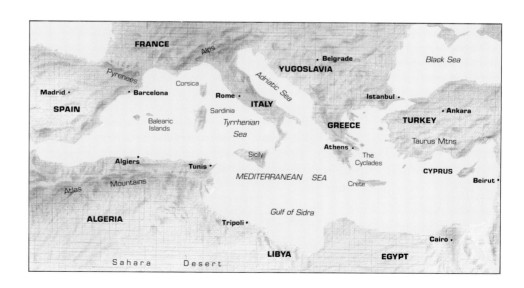

Other smaller species tended towards comparatively larger sizes than their continental counterparts. This was particularly the case with the birds — including the birds of prey.

Two subspecies of *Podarcis*, a lizard, are believed to have disappeared in the 1960s from Ratas in the Balearics and San Stefano in the Tyrrhenian Sea.

The establishment of the large mammals on these islands appears to have resulted from accidental migrations, but it is possible that variations in sea level during the ice ages may have made some periods of settlement possible. Human settlement being early (6000 B.C.), these species are known only from fossils, except for a rodent and a deer.

Birds

Two nocturnal birds of prey, *Speotyto balearica* and *Athene cretensis*, are known only from fossils. These birds were much larger than the present-day species of the same genera. Also, their powers of flight must have been very limited because of their reduced wings; and in the case of the Cretan owl, its talons were very worn at the tips, suggesting that the bird often moved about on the ground, probably by hopping. These nocturnal birds of prey must have been more than 2 feet (60 centimeters) tall, and very probably lived on rodents and insectivores. Their disappearance is thought to have resulted from the elimination of their prey by human agency.

Mammals

The shrew, *Nesiotites*, several species of which are known from the Western Mediterranean, was also to disappear shortly after the arrival of the first humans. *N. corsicanus* became extinct in Corsica during the third millenium, and *N. similis* in Sardinia and *N. hidalgo* in the Balearics more than 6000 years ago.

The Cretan owl, *Athene cretensis*, was a big bird but clearly was able to fly only short distances, for its talons show heavy wear that is attributed to its walking on the ground.

The Balearics owl, *Speotyto balearica*, was also a large bird, probably over 2 feet (60 centimeters) tall. It disappeared not long after the arrival of the first human on its island territories.

Perhaps the most remarkable species on the Mediterranean islands was the pygmy elephant, *Elephas falconeri*, once plentiful in Sicily. Some accounts seem to indicate this animal survived until the Greek era, and even the Roman, but it is in fact known only from bones gathered in caves. It was related to the African elephants, and similar in appearance, but was only 3–5 feet (90–140 centimeters) tall. It was only one-hundredth the weight of its African relatives, making it undoubtedly the most remarkable example of dwarfing in these islands.

These elephants may explain the myth of the roc, the giant bird that was said to feed on elephants, taking them in its talons and lifting them up into the skies before letting them fall to their deaths. It has been said that these legends, which are to be found in *Sinbad the Sailor*, the *Travels of Marco Polo*, and the *Thousand and One Nights*, are about the elephant birds of Madagascar, but they could in fact have a source much closer to Europe.

A species of deer belonging to the genus *Megaceros* also lived on Corsica and Sardinia, where it was exterminated by Neolithic man.

A pygmy subspecies of deer endemic to Corsica, *Cervus elaphus corsicanus*, was first described by Polybius in the second century B.C. A map dating from 1560 shows a dog chasing the deer. Towards the end of the 16th century, several hunters' accounts ask for arquebuses to hunt the deer with, because of claims that they were devastating cultivated fields. In the 17th century, the hunters had adopted the system of driving the deer towards the sea and, once they were in the water, catching them from boats by seizing their antlers. Buffon, the famous naturalist, who raised one in his zoo, stated that the Corsican deer was only half the height of an ordinary deer; it had a brown coat, a squat body, and short legs. However, in 1736 Buffon declared that the deer he had raised had become as

The most unusual animal in the Mediterranean was undoubtedly the dwarf elephant of Sicily, *Elephas falconeri*, that stood only 3–5 feet (1–1.6 meters) high — a runt alongside its African cousins.

big as a French deer, so the dwarfing of the Corsican subspecies seems to have been caused more by the environment than by genetic drift. Unfortunately, the Corsican deer is not well known. In 1965, only four individuals, two of them young, were known, and although in the 1970s there were occasional sightings and about 1980 claims that there were still some 15 left, it seems probable that today the deer has completely disappeared.

Crete had a very diverse deer population. No fewer than seven species belonging to two endemic genera have been recognized. *Megaceros cretensis* had very large antlers, yet its body was no larger than the European deer of today. All seven species had very short legs.

Deer of the *Candiacervus* genus from Crete, described in 1975, are known only from fossils. They had very peculiar club-shaped antlers. The smallest

A pygmy subspecies of deer endemic to Corsica, *Cervus elaphus corsicanus* was, according to the 18th century naturalist Buffon, 'a basset among deer'.

The Cretan deer included six species. The smallest of the pygmy species of the genus *Candiacervus* stood only 16 inches (40 centimeters) high.

species, *C. ropalophorus*, stood only 16 inches (40 centimeters) tall, whereas the antlers could be as long as 31 inches (79 centimeters). Other species could reach the size of modern deer, which they resembled closely except, again, for their short legs. Neolithic man is considered to have caused their disappearance in a few centuries through hunting and cultivation of the land.

The 'rat-rabbit' or pika of Corsica, *Prolagus corsicanus*, was a strange animal, in appearance halfway between a guinea-pig and a rabbit. Rather a squat animal, it had hind legs that were better developed than those of the rabbit. Its ears were probably round, and its massive head made it look more like a guinea-pig. Most of the bones found in Corsica bear witness to the hunting of these unusual animals. The bones from the extremities of the limbs, and the muzzle, usually show signs of heat damage, suggesting that they were cooked on a spit. Because they are the most plentiful species in the archeological deposits, they appear to have been a favorite quarry. Apart from the texts mentioning this species, it is known only from bones, and was described by Cuvier in 1823. The rat-rabbit hunted by Neolithic man was described by Polybius (202–120 B.C.), who called it *kuniklos*. It survived quite late; traces of the existence of the Sardinian species, *Prolagus sardus*, occur up to 1777 on the islet of Tavolara off the northeast coast.

Three species of rodent, the doormouse *Hypnomys morpheus* on the Balearics, and the field mouse *Rhagamys orthodon* and vole *Tyrrhenicola henseli* on Corsica and Sardinia, have also disappeared, it is thought shortly after the arrival of humans.

The Mediterranean rodent *Prolagus*, half way between a rabbit and a guinea-pig, must have made a big contribution to the food of the first human inhabitants of the islands.

There used to be three species of the Balearics 'cave goats,' *Myotragus*, and some were domesticated. This is a rare example of a domesticated animal that has not survived.

Hippopotamuses, that now survive only in Africa, used to have many relatives on some Mediterranean islands. All these forms were pygmy ones, and their extinctions appear to have resulted from hunting and the destruction of their natural environment.

An unusual carnivore, *Cynotherium sardous*, lived in Sardinia, and probably disappeared soon after humans arrived there. This species resembled a dog and was the largest carnivorous mammal of these islands.

There has not yet been any discovery of its remains in association with humans. Its origins may go back to the Tertiary era.

A genus peculiar to the Balearics, the goat *Myotragus*, included three species. It also was an unusual, short-legged mammal with some features making it look like a goat, in particular the very forward location of the eyes on the face, so that it would only have been able to see out to its sides. *Myotragus* stood only about 20 inches (50 centimeters) high at the shoulder — not much larger than a newborn kid. It must have been very agile, able to climb the precipitous cliffs of the islands, as is shown by the various modifications of its skeleton. It appears to have been hunted, because broken and charred bones have been found. It seems, moreover, that this species was partially domesticated, because of thick deposits of its excreta found in caves, corresponding to the penning of several animals. *Myotragus* is a rare example of a domesticated animal that has now disappeared.

Europe
In the Time of the Hunter Kings

The early human settlement of Europe is proven by the discovery in the commune of Chilhac (Haute-Loire, France) of tools two million years old. They were found alongside the remains of a mastodon. They are the earliest European human evidence known and they also bear witness to the hunting of the great mammals.

Europe is also the homeland of modern humans, *Homo sapiens*. More primitive forms of course appeared there, for example Tautavel man, who lived 450,000 years ago in the eastern Pyrenees. Neanderthal man, *Homo sapiens neanderthalensis*, discovered for the first time in a cave in Germany, lived over almost all of Europe. Appearing about 200,000 years ago, these humans did not survive for long after the arrival 40,000 years ago of Cro-Magnon man, the first *Homo sapiens sapiens*. The evolution of new tools, hunting techniques and mode of thought can be followed better in Europe than in other parts of the world.

The environment has been profoundly modified since the first human settlement; for example, the many successive ice ages have each brought about great changes in the composition of the flora and fauna.

The pardine lynx of Spain, *Felis lynx pardina*, the bison *Bison bonasus*, and Audouin's gull, *Larus audouinii*, are among the most endangered species in Europe.

The lion was one of the first to vanish. Once abundant in Greece, as the accounts of the ancients show, it survived only for a short time after humans came on the scene.

A small wild pansy, *Viola cryana*, peculiar to the upper basin of the Seine in France, was discovered in 1860 on the chalky screes of the Armançon valley. Quarrying seems to be responsible for the extinction of this species, which does not appear to have survived in cultivation after 1950.

Birds

Man has caused the disappearance of few bird species in Europe. Some, like the crane *Grus primigenia*, described by Alphonse Milne-Edwards, may have been hunted by Cro-Magnon man, but climatic changes may provide a better explanation for its disappearance.

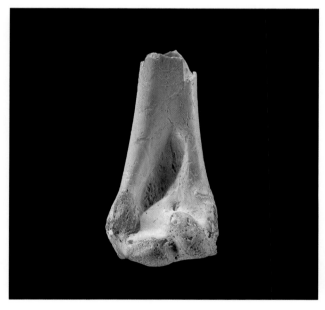

The crane, rediscovered at French prehistoric sites, is known only from its limb-bones.

Mammals

The mammoth, *Mammuthus primigenius*, was hunted all over the Continent. This gigantic mastodon, that stood over 16 feet (5 meters) high, must have represented a large part of the food supply of prehistoric humans, for its bones have been found in abundance on most sites. Its tusks provided ivory from which the first statuettes were carved. The oldest known boomerang — that is European, not Australian — was cut from a mammoth tusk. In the east, where the mammoth was to survive longer, thanks to the rigorous climate that suited the animal, the bones and tusks were used to build shelters. Arranged in a circle so that each supported the other, they were then covered with skins.

We have many examples of mammoth remains, and not only bones. The Siberian ice has preserved many frozen animals, and a baby mammoth was discovered about 10 years ago. The quality of mammoth preservation is such that one expedition that had run out of food was able to make several meals of the meat from one of the bodies they discovered, without

Prehistoric humans used the bones and tusks of the mammoth to build homes.

The European mammoth was for many years hunted for its meat. This is the frozen specimen exhibited in St Petersburg in 1804.

any ill effects. An animal that had disappeared more than 1000 years ago was thus able to save the lives of the men and dogs of this expedition.

The remarkable state of preservation of these remains has fostered the hope among Soviet scientists of recreating the species by placing the genetic material from a mammoth cell in an elephant ovule (egg cell), and then placing the ovule in the uterus of an elephant.

The aurochs, *Bos primigenius*, is one of the most famous extinct animals. Our ancestors knew it well since they painted it on a number of cave walls, hunted it, ate it, carved its bones and shaped its skin to make tools

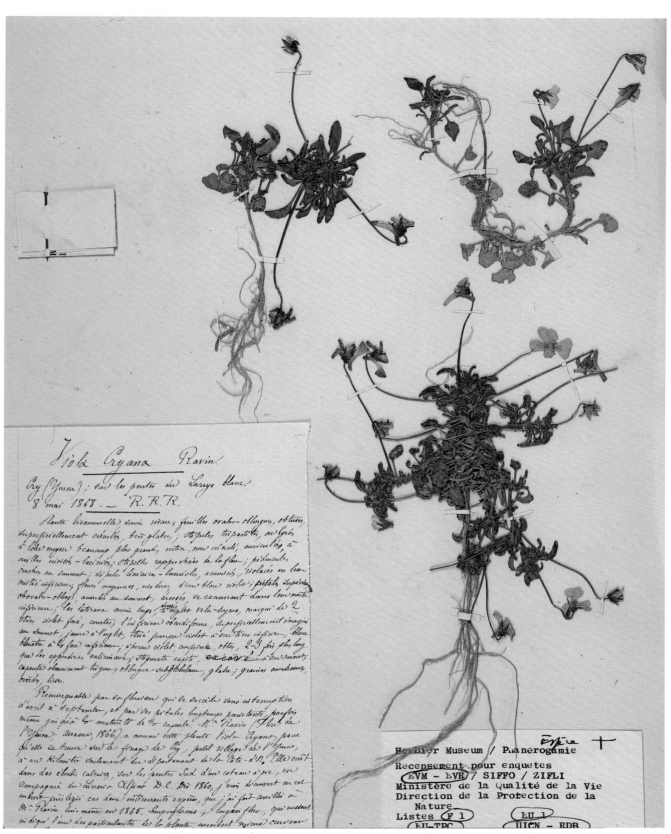

A wild violet, *Viola cryana*, endemic to the Paris basin in France, disappeared before the end of last century.

or clothes. This primitive ox stood more than 6½ feet (2 meters) high, and had spiral horns that could reach a length of 32 inches (81 centimeters). Appearing in India half a million years ago, it disappeared in 1627. It lived in small herds comprising a bull, several females, and calves. Apart from the wolf, which no doubt killed calves that had strayed from the herd, the aurochs' main enemy was humans.

As far back as the first century B.C., Caesar tells of the hunt by the Germanic tribes in his famous *De Bello Gallico*. The Gauls hunted the aurochs, and from the Middle Ages come many similar accounts. Charlemagne, Louis the Debonair, Lotharius, and many others regarded

The cave bear, *Ursus spelaeus*, was a peaceful vegetarian.

it as their favorite quarry. In the 16th century, when the aurochs disappeared in France, Conrad Gessner wrote about the hunt:

> One individual is separated from the herd and hunted by many men and dogs, often for a long time. It falls only when hit in the chest. While it is still alive the skin between the horns is torn off and sent, along with the heart and both fresh and salt meat, to the king. He sometimes sends it as a present to other princes.

According to some authors, the aurochs was half domesticated towards the end of the 16th century. Because of the growing rarity of this princely game, at the request of the local nobility the last aurochs of the Jaktorov Forest near Warsaw were herded together in an enclosure so they could be watched over by guards and fed during the winter. In 1564 eight solitary old bulls still survived, along with 22 old cows, three young bulls and five calves. Of the 25 animals remaining in 1599, only four were left in 1602, and the last cow died in 1627.

Since the beginning of this century, there have been several attempts to re-create the aurochs, resulting in a breed that bears a strange resemblance to the cave paintings but only superficially resembles the extinct animal.

The aurochs, *Bos primigenius*, disappeared in 1627.

Bison priscus disappeared because our ancestors hunted it.

The European bison, *Bison bonasus*, often confused with the aurochs, has today become very scarce. Only the Polish subspecies has survived. The Caucasian subspecies, *Bison bonasus caucasicus*, described in 1906, has disappeared. The Czars presided over its fate. In 1805 there were about 400 left, but World War I and the October Revolution removed all imperial authority over the protection of the animals, and in the wild the bison were massacred. In 1915 important protective measures were taken, including the establishment of a reserve by forcibly moving the people living on the piece of land involved. This caused great dissatisfaction because their pasturelands were considered to be a heritage handed down from time immemorial. The bison at this point numbered only about 100. By 1921 they had dwindled to about 50 and in 1923 only 15–20 were left. It seems that the dispossessed people had whenever possible taken their 'revenge' by killing all bison they met with. In 1924 the Soviet Government set up the Kuban Reserve. Three years later, no living bison remained; two carcasses were found, both showing evidence that their deaths had not been by natural causes.

The last known representative of this subspecies, an old bull called 'Caucasus,' died at the age of 18 on February 26, 1925. The Czar himself had given it to a Hamburg animal trader, Karl Hagenbeck. About 10 animals of the Polish subspecies are thought to descend from this bull and to have some of the genetic stock of the Caucasian form. There have been some attempts, by back-crossings, to re-create the extinct subspecies.

The cave bear, *Ursus spelaeus*, that lived at the same time as the Neanderthals and Cro-Magnons, was essentially vegetarian, and like most bears it hibernated for many months of the year. This feature undoubtedly inspired the first cults, since many bones have been found in caves, such as the Regourdou Cave in the Dordogne, in France. The skulls, femurs and tibias were carefully sorted and laid in rows. Men may have associated the idea of resurrection with the deep sleep of the bear during the winter and its reawakening in spring. The Regourdou Cave, no doubt the oldest sign of some form of cult, was inhabited by Neanderthal man. The impressively large cave bear was in fact a peaceful animal; it was usually vegetarian, and seems to have hunted only the salmon that came up the streams.

The cave lion was very plentiful during the age of prehistoric humans, and may have survived into the Greek era, when there is mention that it existed in Thrace and Macedonia, unless we are dealing with a form close to the African *Panthera leo*.

The Pyrenean ibex, once very numerous, included at least two subspecies. One of these, *Capra pyrenaica pyrenaica*, could still exist, although the rare survivors may be crossbreeds. *C. pyrenaica lusitanica* is thought to have disappeared in 1892. The horns of this ibex could reach more than 3 feet (1 meter), although the body size was comparable to that of a wild goat. It was certainly a fine trophy, and said to have therapeutic qualities that were highly prized by medieval people.

The Irish elk, *Cervus megaceros*, was certainly the most impressive of the Cervidae, with its antlers having a spread sometimes greater than

This subspecies of the Pyrenean ibex, *Capra pyrenaica lusitanica*, was intensively hunted in medieval times.

The antlers of the biggest European deer, *Cervus megaceros*, had a spread of more than 6 feet (2 meters).

6½ feet (2 meters). Although its habitat extended over most of Europe, it seems that its last refuge was in the north of England and Ireland. Abundant remains of this large deer are found in peat bogs, and occur as well in caves inhabited by humans, who also painted it. This animal became extinct in about the 9th millenium B.C.

Africa
Land of Wild Beasts

Today's African fauna includes many of the currently most endangered species of the world.

The elephant is a well-known example. Every year, 40–60,000 are slaughtered, and the total African elephant population is of the order of 600,000. Some say they have only about 10 years left, while others contend that elephant herds are too numerous, and several countries regularly set about controlling their numbers.

'White gold,' as ivory is called, is the main reason for the slaughter. The poacher sells the ivory for less than U.S.$10 per kilo, but by the time the ivory reaches the purchasing countries it fetches about $80 per kilo. The animal's meat and skin become dust, its tusks are turned into billiard balls, necklaces, and other ornaments. What makes it all even more tragic is that so many of the animals killed are young ones with only about one-third the ivory of an adult. The international CITES convention, which

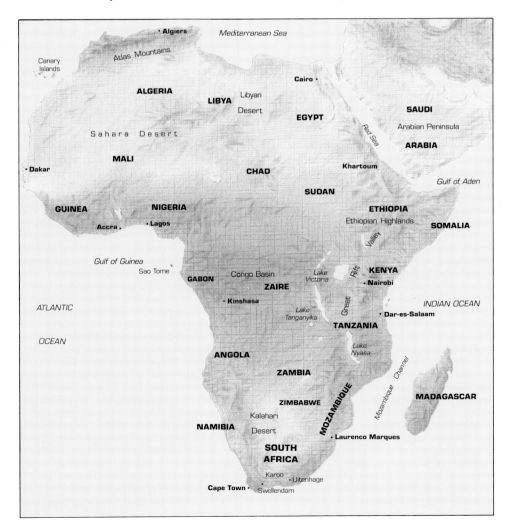

Initiation rite for African lion hunters, based on a description by Dr. David Livingstone in his book.

seeks to control the trade in endangered species, makes special mention of a ban on commercial uses of ivory.

Among the most endangered species in Africa today are the gorilla, *Gorilla gorilla*, the addax antelope, *Addax nasomaculatus*, the bontebok, *Damaliscus dorcas dorcas*, and the Ethiopian ibex, *Capra walie*.

Africa is the cradle of humanity. *Australopithecus*, the first known human, lived there more than 3 million years ago; *Homo habilis* about 2 million years ago, then *Homo erectus*. Human evolution occurred through the appearance of more highly evolved forms replacing more primitive forms. So the first remains of a robust *Australopithecus* were found just a short distance from the first known *Homo habilis* remains (including tools). It is no big step to suppose that they met in conflict, or even that the more evolved ate the more primitive.

The African continent has already experienced the extinction of a large number of species, often too long ago for the role of humans, who had only very rudimentary weapons, to be established beyond doubt. For many species, climatic changes and the appearance of new predators seem to be the main causes of extinction.

Africa had a remarkable example of a refuge zone in the Atlas region, which underwent change later than the other North African areas and provided shelter for about a dozen species and subspecies that have since become extinct.

Birds

Only two African bird species are so far accepted as extinct. The nightjar, *Caprimulgus ludovicianus*, is known only from a specimen collected in Ethiopia. It appears to have died out at the beginning of this century. The finch, *Neospiza concolor*, is thought to have disappeared in the early 1900s. It lived on the island of São Tomé, off the Guinea coast. Only two specimens are known.

Mammals

A subspecies of squirrel, close to *Epixerus ebii*, was described in 1853 from a specimen from Liberia. It is considered to have disappeared around the beginning of this century, as the result of habitat destruction.

The African Equidae have lost two distinct forms, both zebras, in less than a century. The quagga, *Equus quagga*, was an ancestral form of zebra that lived in South Africa. It was very aggressive and was often used among the herds of cattle to act as a guard, warning of the arrival of intruders even if it did not directly attack them. A few quaggas were exported to England, and some even became harness horses. Quaggas became extinct all the more rapidly because of their confined habitat. When the Boers settled in South Africa, the quagga was hunted as game to feed servants and workers, to get skins and leather for their homes, and even for export. The last wild quagga was killed in 1878, and the very last one of all died in 1883 in the Amsterdam Zoo.

Burchell's zebra, *Equus burchelli*, disappeared about 1910. Its habitat overlapped with the quagga's, and many people wanted to regard it as the quagga stallion. However, the two species clearly had distinct coats, that of the quagga being browner with few stripes on the back, and Burchell's zebra having white legs and tail. Naturalists do not agree on whether

Burchell's zebra was for a long time regarded as the male of the quagga.

Despite the establishment of a farm-raised herd, the Cape hartebeeste, *Alcelaphus caama caama*, died out. This drawing was made by Anders Warren, the naturalist on Cook's second voyage, in 1774.

Burchell's zebra was a distinct species from the modern one, and there are many specimens with oddly light-colored legs and tail.

A subspecies of bubal, the bubal hartebeeste, *Alcelaphus buselaphus buselaphus*, used to live in North Africa, from Egypt to Morocco. At the beginning of this century it occurred only in the Atlas mountains. The last specimen killed in the wild fell in 1902 in Algeria, but the last representative of the subspecies is thought to have died in captivity, in Paris during 1923. However, evidence also suggests that a few individuals may have survived up to 1925 in Morocco.

The Cape hartebeeste, *Alcelaphus caama caama*, was to disappear in South Africa because of hunting and dogs. This gazelle was plentiful around Cape Town in about 1800, but the slaughter was to cause its rapid near-disappearance, since in 1833 there were only 25 left in Natal. In fact, the few survivors were shut up on a farm whose owners had decided to keep them away from the hunt and the attacks of dogs. They lasted more than a century on that same farm, numbering 55 head in 1938 when the farm was sold and the herd set loose. There may, however, be a few hybrid descendants still surviving.

The blue antelope of South Africa, *Hippotragus leucophaeus*, was probably the first African species to disappear because of the white settlers, in about 1799. The first white settlers called it the blue goat because of its resemblance to the goats, in particular its goatee beard and its curved horns, and because of its blue-gray color. The first scientific description of this species goes back to 1766. Its distribution seems to have already been reduced to the Swellendam region when those first colonists came. Hunting was apparently very easy, as the animal was not timid and could easily be approached. Its meat was mainly used as dog food. In 1799, Lichtenstein wrote in his *Travels* that the last animals had recently been killed and their skins sent to Leiden. Many skins of this species are supposed to have reached Europe, but there appear to be only five left in the world. The blue antelope was for a long time confused with other antelopes, but is in fact a distinct species, differing from its relatives in size, shape of horns, and the color of its coat. The last six specimens were observed in 1796.

Megalotragus was a giant antelope that disappeared during the Holocene. Some of its remains have been found in deposits of an age that suggests humans hunted it. However, the climatic changes that occurred in Africa during the Quaternary could have played a major role in its extinction.

Sivatherium, a close relation of the giraffe, is known only from fossils. Humans were contemporary with this animal and seem to have hunted it, because of the association of its bones with traces of human origin, and a few cave paintings. As with *Megalotragus*, climate changes during the Quaternary may be implicated in its extinction.

The Barbary lion, *Panthera leo leo*, belongs to a subspecies that has been extinct since 1922. This is the lion to which Christians were thrown by the Romans, and it is a very close relative of today's 'king of the jungle.' Along with the Cape lion it was the largest of all lions. Its impressive mane covered half its body. The male could weigh as much as 500 pounds (227 kilograms) and measured 10 feet (3 meters) from nose to tail. This cat was well known to the Roman world; Caesar alone owned more than 100 of them and Nero no doubt had a few more. These man-eaters were raised for the games in the arenas and for the torment of Christians. Their habitat once covered most of North Africa. During the colonization of that area, the Barbary lion was already restricted to Tunisia, Algeria, and Morocco. In Libya, the last known lion was killed about 1700, and the last Algerian and Tunisian ones in 1891. A few lions may have lived on after that year, since some accounts mention their existence up to 1899.

In 1861 and 1862 one of these lions, 'obedient as a sheep,' made the headlines in the *Moniteur de l'Algérie*. Led by two natives through the streets of Algiers, it took part in a collection for the brotherhood of Si Mohammed ben-Aouda. In 1862, General Marguerite declared that the average number of animals killed was no greater than three or four a year. Before the French came, the Thoks encouraged the Arabs to exterminate

The blue antelope, *Hippotragus leucophaeus*, was probably the first African vertebrate to become extinct at the hand of humans. Its meat was mainly fed to dogs.

them, exonerating from all taxes the two tribes who hunted the lion, the Ouled Meloul and the Ouled Cessi, as well as paying them handsomely for the skins.

When the rarity of this animal became public knowledge, many foreigners came to seek fame and fortune by hunting it. So the *Portraits of MM. Chassaing and Bombonnel, the two slayers of wild beasts* were the subject of an exhibition by the painter Girardin in December 1865. These two men were also productive authors, and published *Bombonnel, Slayer of Panthers: his hunting exploits recounted by himself* in 1864; and *My Lion Hunts*, by Chassaing, published in 1865. When the French invaded Tunis in 1881, the Barbary lion still seemed plentiful, and a few groups appeared to be still surviving in southern Algeria in 1899. In that year A.E. Pease, an Algerian resident, wrote that the Algerian lion had become close to extinction.

Sivatherium was a close relative of the giraffe. The animal is known only from fossils, but it would appear that humans used to hunt it.

Algerian Government figures record the decrease in the lion numbers. In 1878, 28 were officially killed; 22 in 1879; 16 in 1880; 6 in 1881; 4 in 1882; 3 in 1883; and 1 in 1884. Its last refuge was in the Central Atlas mountains, in particular in the territories of the Zaian and Beni M'guild tribes. This region still had plenty of trees, and remained one of the wildest. The last members of this formidable species undoubtedly were finished off after the civil wars and banditry in Morocco prompted the introduction of firearms.

Megalotragus was a giant antelope.

Tartarin of Tarascon's Lion

On the right loomed up confusedly the heavy mass of a mountain — perhaps the Atlas range. On the heart-hand the invisible sea hollowly rolling. The very spot to attract wild beasts.

With one gun laid before him and the other in his grasp, Tartarin of Tarascon went down on one knee and waited an hour, ay, a good couple, and nothing turned up. Then he bethought him how, in his books, the great lion-slayers never went out hunting without having a lamb or a kid along with them, that they tied up a space before them, and set bleating or baa-ing by jerking its foot with a string. Not having any goat, the Tarasconer had the idea of employing an imitation, and he set to crying in a tremulous voice, —

'Baa-a-a!'

At first it was done very softly, because at bottom he was a little alarmed lest the lion should hear him; but as nothing came, he baa-ed more loudly. Still nothing. Losing patience, he resumed many times running at the top of his voice, till the 'Baa, baa, baa!' came out with so much power that the goat began to be mistakable for a bull.

Unexpectedly, a few steps in front, some gigantic black thing appeared. He was hushed. This thing lowered its head, sniffed the ground, bounded up, rolled over, and darted off at the gallop, but returned and stopped short. Who could doubt it was the lion? for now its four short legs could plainly be seen, its formidable mane and its large eyes gleaming in the gloom.

Up went his gun into position. Fire's the word! and bang, bang! it was done.

— Alphonse Daudet

The Cape lion, *Panthera leo melanochaitus*, a different subspecies, is thought to have died out in South Africa about 1865. It was described in 1846 as having the head of a bulldog, a black mane and a tuft of black hair under the belly. The enormous black mane and the black hair bordering the edges of its ears were particularly striking. In 1800 it still inhabited the Karoo, the Uitenhage, and even the environs of Cape Town. A stuffed specimen, killed in 1836, is preserved in London. Some hunters claimed that it ate antelopes, zebras, giraffes and buffalo. The last known specimen was killed by General Bisset in Natal in 1865. Dr Livingstone himself was attacked by a lion during his exploration of the Cape Colony. If the animal was a Cape lion, it must have been one of the last. Other accounts mention the many incidents this now-extinct animal caused.

The Atlas bear, *Ursus arctos crowtheri*, has a similar history to that of the Barbary lion. It became progressively reduced in distribution, first as a result of habitat destruction and later at the hands of hunters with firearms. Two specimens were sent to France, one of them being given

The Barbary lion was kept by Cæsar and Nero for the arena games and the torment of Christians. Its habitat once covered most of North Africa, but it is a subspecies that has been extinct since 1922.

to the Marseilles Zoo in 1830 by the Emperor of Morocco. This species was to find refuge in the Atlas mountains before disappearing about 1870.

Another formidable carnivore, the sabre-toothed tiger, *Meganthereon*, mingled with the first men, but the causes of its disappearance remain a puzzle; climatic changes may have played a role, but the growing scarcity of its prey, that man also hunted, may well have contributed greatly to its extinction.

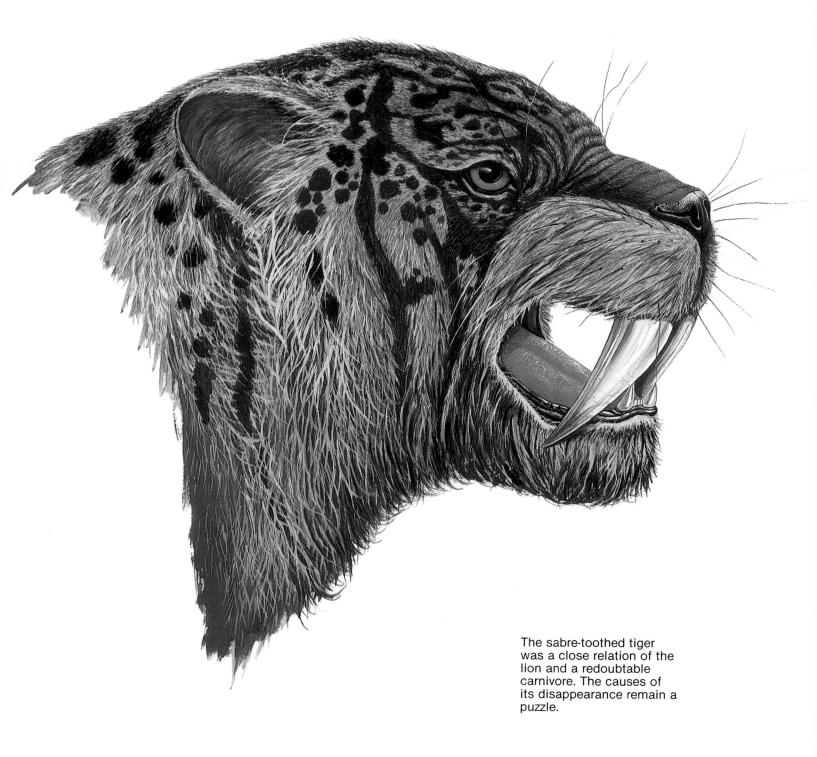

The sabre-toothed tiger was a close relation of the lion and a redoubtable carnivore. The causes of its disappearance remain a puzzle.

Asia
The Tiger and the Frog

The Asian fauna seems quite well preserved in comparison to many other regions of the world. However, several animals, the panda *Ailuropoda melanoleuca*, the tiger *Panthera tigris*, the Java rhinoceros *Rhinoceros sondaicus*, the Arabian antelope *Oryx leucoryx*, the snow leopard *Panthera uncia*, and the orangutan *Pongo pygmaeus* are among the best known endangered species.

The rhinoceroses have been hunted for centuries for their horns, the price of which has reached half their weight in gold.

The Asian lion, *Panthera leo persicus*, that inhabited the Near and Middle East until the beginning of last century, is now found only in the Gir Forest of the Kathiawar Peninsula in India, where fewer than 200 animals still survive.

The Arabian oryx seems doomed as long as man continues to hunt it in vehicles. The antelope *Saiga tatarica*, once intensively hunted, seems to have acquired a new lease of life as a result of the protective measures taken on its behalf.

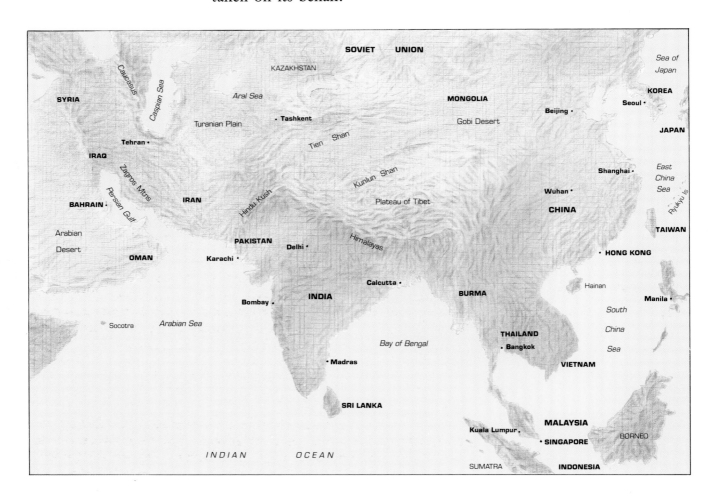

Antelope-hunting scene in Iran.

The Przewalski horses (Mongolian wild horses) now exist only in zoos, and the onager and hemionus (Asiatic wild asses) run the risk of suffering the same fate in the near future.

Finally the panda, a world symbol of nature preservation, appears condemned to die out despite the tremendous efforts made by the Chinese biologists and Government.

Amphibians

The Palestinian painted frog, *Discoglossus nigriventer*, used to inhabit Lake Hula on the Israeli-Syrian border. It was not discovered until 1940, and disappeared in 1956, a victim of drainage and wetlands modification. Five specimens have been collected, two tadpoles and two young in 1940, and an adult female in 1955. The two young were placed in a terrarium, but the larger, a female, wasted no time before devouring her partner. The adult female, the last known representative of the species, survived some time in a terrarium.

Birds

The ostrich, largest of the contemporary running birds, has not in the past been confined solely to Africa. Two other forms are known; one from Syria and Arabia, and one from China. The first, *Struthio camelus syriacus*, was commonly encountered up to the beginning of World War

I. Ostrich feathers were then in very great demand, and the war had meant a large numbers of firearms were suddenly in circulation. The end came with World War II when a specimen was killed in Bahrein in 1941, and the last one was killed and eaten by a German tank crew during 1944.

The Chinese ostrich, *Struthio asiaticus*, is known only from subfossil eggshell fragments and mentioned in early imperial writings. These latter mention the last one, eaten at an imperial meal during the Third Dynasty.

Jerdon's courser, *Rhinoptilus bitorquatus*, lived in eastern India, but its disappearance went almost unnoticed. Described in 1848, its last sighting for many years was in 1900. The searches did not begin until 50 years later; at first fruitless, they have recently resulted in the rediscovery of the bird, that is surviving in very small numbers.

Blewitt's owl, *Athene blewitti*, of central India, was last observed in 1914. The last known specimen was killed by a German ornithologist near Bombay. Searches undertaken in 1975 by the famous American ornithologist, Sir Dillon Ripley, were unsuccessful. Its disappearance appears to have resulted from the destruction of the forests it lived in.

The pink-headed duck, *Rhodonessa caryophyllacea*, was discovered at the end of the 18th century. It lived in the lower basins of the Ganges and Brahmaputra Rivers, measured about 2 feet (60 centimeters), and laid white eggs that were remarkable for their perfectly spherical form. Although rarely remembered by ornithologists, this bird is still represented by 80 specimens in world collections. Calcutta seems to have had the greatest concentration of these ducks. In the 1890s, no fewer than half a dozen were daily put on sale during the winter markets. They were bought alive,

The painted frog, *Discoglossus nigriventer*, is known only from five specimens, two of them tadpoles; all died in the laboratory while under study.

as ornamental birds, because their meat was not highly esteemed. In 1915 none were any longer available at the market, despite an offer of nearly seven times the usual price. The last known representative in India was observed in 1935, and no subsequent search has been able to locate the bird. Some captive ducks are said to have survived in England, in Foxwarren Park, and at Clères in France. About a dozen birds have been recorded there, but none reproduced. This species was lost mainly through drainage and transformation of wetlands.

The crested shelduck, *Tadorna cristata*, once plentiful in Korea, is known only from three specimens. The first one with which Europeans became acquainted was captured in 1877. It was a female, and is now preserved in Holland. Rare specimens, taken in 1914, and the last in 1916, were sold to the Japanese, who had known of the bird since the 1850s.

The Himalayan mountain quail, *Ophrysia superciliosa*, belongs to a genus that is endemic to this high-altitude mountainous region. The dozen specimens preserved were taken from sites between 5000–7000 feet (1500—2300 meters) altitude, making them the highest-dwelling of any extinct birds. Some were kept at lower altitude, in the private zoo of the Count of Derby. Last observed in 1868, these quail lived on grasses, insects and berries. Why they disappeared remains obscure. They were seen only infrequently, and environmental changes that may have affected them are not fully understood.

Jerdon's courser, *Rhinoptilus bitorquatus*, was an Indian bird considered extinct from 1900. Fifty years later a search located a few remaining survivors.

The Miyako kingfisher, *Halcyon miyakoensis*, unique to the Ryukyu Islands, is known from a single specimen killed in 1887. Although it was not very well preserved, this bird is apparently distinguished from its relatives by the color of its feathers and its red legs.

The giant heron, *Ardea bennuides*, a close relative of the present-day gray heron, was discovered in 1974 during archeological excavations in the Sultanate of Oman, and was described by Swedish scientists. It is the largest species of its genus, estimated at nearly 6 feet (2 meters) from the single tibia fragment that was found. The circumstances of its discovery suggest that this bird was regularly hunted. Naturalists have never observed it alive.

Mammals

An Israeli gerbil is thought to have become extinct in 1986. Its seaside habitat was reduced to a single site where the construction of a complex of dwellings caused its disappearance.

The Bali tiger, *Panthera tigris balica*, was the smallest of the tigers and the only subspecies so far to have died out, although today all tigers are seriously endangered in the wild. Still numerous at the beginning of the century, the Bali tiger was on the verge of extinction in 1935, at the time

The pink-headed duck, *Rhodonessa caryophyllacea*, was sold in the Calcutta market as an ornamental bird. It never reproduced in captivity and died out in 1935.

Blewitt's owl, *Athene blewitti*, disappeared after
the destruction of its forest habitat.

of a report for the Commission on the Protection of Nature. Because of the systematic hunting it had suffered, there were only a few left in the west of Bali, and the last one, a female, was killed in 1937. Extinction of Bali tigers resulted from the introduction of firearms, along with the excessive desire for them as trophies — although they were quite insignificant as tiger trophies go.

Japan used to have two wolf species. The smaller, *Canis lupus hodophylax*, called *shamanu* by the Japanese, was described by Temminck as a separate species. It was the smallest species of wolf ever known, measuring just over 3 feet (1 meter). The Japanese hunted it down because they feared it and because its skin could be sold for a good price. The Sapporo Government in 1888 even offered up to 10 yen per skin. The last known shamanu was killed in 1905, and its skin sold to an English traveler.

A big black bear, *Ursus arctos piscator*, lived until the beginning of this century on the Kamchatka Peninsula. It is known only from a few accounts, especially those of the naturalist Sten Bergman of Stockholm. He was shown a skin of one of these bears, and its size was greater than the biggest bears he had ever seen elsewhere. The Russian hunters

The Himalayan mountain quail, *Ophrysia superciliosa*, lived at sites between 5–7000 feet (1600–2300 meters), the highest altitude of any known extinct bird.

confirmed this account, having killed some that weighed up to 1500 pounds (680 kilograms). This gigantic black bear disappeared about 1920.

Schomburgk's deer, *Cervus schomburgki*, lived in Thailand. One stuffed specimen and several heads with antlers are preserved around the world, but the species has died out without any Western naturalist having been able to observe it in its natural environment. A single live specimen (today preserved in the Gallery of Extinct Animals at the Natural History Museum in Paris) was shown to the public in 1867 in the Jardin des Plantes, 5 years after its discovery. During the 70 years between its discovery and its extinction, nearly 200 skins were sold, but this deer was hunted less for its skin than for its velvet, to which the Chinese attributed many medicinal qualities. The deer frequented the marshes, moving from island to island, and the hunters harpooned it from boats. Draining of the marshes and cultivation of the land caused it to become extremely rare; and the peasants with their firearms hastened its disappearance.

Two Asian species of Equidae disappeared. The Syrian hemippus was the smallest of the asses, standing about 3 feet (1 meter) high, but was also the boldest and swiftest. It used to live in Syria, Palestine, Arabia, and ancient Mesopotamia. Hunting of it occurred very early, since King

The Bali tiger, *Panthera tigris balica*, is the only subspecies of tiger to have disappeared as a result of hunting, but the other forms are all endangered today.

The shamanu or Japanese wolf, *Canis lupus hodophylax*, was the smallest wolf ever known.

Assurbanipal took an active part, as can be seen on bas-reliefs dating from 650 B.C. Because of its size and its wild nature, this ass was not successfully domesticated but instead hunted for meat. It does seem, however, that in the 16th century some nomads did domesticate a few females for their milk. Because it was difficult to capture in the desert, some hunters pursued only the young, which were easier to catch. The introduction of firearms during World War I, and of vehicles that were faster than camels and generally more practical for chasing an animal on the run, sealed the fate of this species. In 1930 some naturalists and the nomad peoples still hoped to rediscover this species, but it seems that the last wild specimen was killed in 1927 while drinking at the Al Ghams Oasis. The last one of all, a specimen in a zoo, died the following year.

The tarpan, *Equus ferus gmelini*, was a pony from Eastern Europe and Asia. It also roamed the Ukrainian and Mongolian steppes and the Gobi desert. It was used as a draught animal by trappers and mammoth-ivory hunters in Siberia. The last known one living in the wild was killed in Russia on Christmas Day, 1879, and the last animal in captivity, in Poland, died in 1887. Only then, unfortunately, did the Polish Government try to revive the species, placing in reserves some wild horses that still possessed features of the tarpan. The few zoo specimens bearing this name today are merely the results of reverse crossbreeding from the few hybrid wild animals it was possible to capture.

This wild ass from Syria, *Equus hemionus hemippus*, stood only about 3 feet (90 centimeters) at the shoulder. As well as being smallest, it was also boldest and swiftest of the asses, but to little avail, for the last specimen died in 1928.

Australia
Marsupials and Aborigines

This vast continent, more than 2.9 million square miles (7.6 million square kilometers) in area, and isolated from neighboring continents since the middle of the Tertiary era, is home to a unique and very ancient fauna of marsupials. These animals have undergone a remarkable evolution, leading to an extraordinary array of species resembling such diverse but not closely related creatures as moles, dogs, hares, and jerboas. Australia is also the homeland of the famous platypus, an egg-laying mammal.

Marsupials are distinct from placental mammals because of the marsupial pouch in which the young are fed and continue their development after being born. There are nearly 250 species of marsupials in Australia.

Australian birds number more than 650 species, including the lyrebird, many parrots, emus, etc.

Exploration of this vast continent began in earnest about 1800, and some of the early explorers met tragic ends. One expedition, after missing several rendezvous to restock with provisions, perished because they could not bring themselves to eat kangaroo meat, even though the many Aborigines who frequented the area had shown them it was edible.

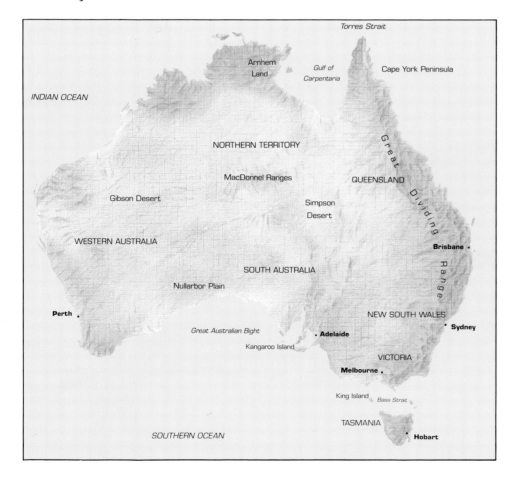

Australian Aborigines with ritual face and body decorations attending a corroboree, and (right) a contemporary Aborigine in the Australian outback.

Australia was first colonized by humans between 40,000 and 36,000 B.C., by Aborigines who travelled on foot across the land bridge from what is now New Guinea. (Torres Strait, that today separates the two countries, was then dry.) The earliest authenticated visit by Europeans was in 1606 by the Dutch ship *Duyfken* under the command of Willem Jansz, although there is evidence of visits by Portuguese navigators in the early 17th century. Tasmania, or Van Diemen's Land, was discovered in 1642 by Abel Tasman.

The 1800s saw many expeditions by naturalists and discoverers. Baudin's French expedition (1800–1803), with 24 scientists in the crew, discovered many new species. John Gould, the famous naturalist and highly talented animal illustrator, devoted the major part of his work to studying the fauna of Australia. Nearly one-third of the kangaroo species he described are today extinct.

The extinct monitor, *Megalania prisca*, at nearly 23 feet (7 meters) long, was comparable with the East Indies Komodo dragon, the largest of all living lizards.

When the Aborigines arrived, there were few native predators; it was the Aborigines themselves who introduced the dingo, Australia's wild dog. The arrival about 1800 of rabbits, firearms, then foxes, etc., caused unprecedented havoc.

Reptiles

Two impressive reptiles have disappeared, both apparently at the hands of humans, because the fossil record proves they existed at the same time. One was a giant boa, *Wonambi naracoortensis*, from southeast Australia. It was a formidable predator, growing to 16 feet (5 meters) long. The other was a giant goanna, *Megalania prisca*, nearly 23 feet (7 meters) long — twice the length and eight times the weight of its nearest living relative, the Komodo dragon of the East Indies (the largest of all living lizards). The date of the fossils of these animals proves they were contemporaneous with humans.

Birds

The Australian emus, or casqueless cassowaries as earlier authors called them, included two island species that died out before 1850. The black emu of King Island, *Dromaius ater*, is known today only by a mounted skeleton and a stuffed specimen in the Natural History Museum in Paris. The last known member of this species died in the Jardin des Plantes in 1824; it was aged 22 years, and had been brought back by the Baudin expedition. It had spent a few years in the Empress Josephine's gardens before being entrusted to the Jardin des Plantes. Other specimens, slightly larger than those from King Island, belong to the species *D. baudinianus*, and have been taken from Kangaroo Island. This species is known only by a mounted skeleton in Paris, and a skin in Geneva. Both are believed to have come from the same animal.

The giant boa, *Wonambi naracoortensis*, was one of Australia's most impressive reptiles.

The black emu of King Island, *Dromaius ater*, was discovered during the Baudin expedition in 1804. This specimen, believed to be the last of the species, died in France at the age of 22.

The emu population of Tasmania is less well known. They differed from the continental form only by their smaller size. During the 19th century, as this bird, much prized as game, grew rarer, emus from the mainland were introduced. These mixed with the island population to the extent that it is often difficult to decide in reading earlier accounts whether hybrids, island emus or continental ones are under discussion. One of the last Tasmanian emus, a female, was drowned in its owner's swimming pool, leaving a few eggs. There was an attempt at artificially hatching them, but it was unsuccessful.

Although the continental emus survive in large numbers, several species of giant birds, the Dromonorthidae family, died out. They could reach 10 feet (3 meters), and rivalled the New Zealand moas and the Malagasy elephant birds. One 10 foot (3 meter) species of *Genyornis* is contemporary with the Aborigines, and is known to us through many deposits of bones and a rock painting.

Two megapodes of an extinct genus disappeared soon after the arrival of the Aborigines, certainly as a result of the introduction of the dingoes. The megapodes are strange, very primitive birds that do not sit on their eggs but lay them in a large mass of vegetation. Decomposition provides the heat necessary for the development of the young.

Two species of parrot described by John Gould have not been recorded since the beginning of this century, and may be extinct. The night parrot, *Geopsittacis occidentalis*, lived in the deserts, while the paradise parrot, *Psephotus pulcherrimus*, was restricted to Queensland.

Tasmanian Humans

Until 1880, Tasmania was inhabited by an Aboriginal population endemic to this large island south of mainland Australia. Today they have totally disappeared, but we do have some accounts and portraits of these people. One of the notable naturalist expeditions to have met the Tasmanians was that led by D'Entrecasteaux. The ships *La Recherche* and *L'Espérance* called there for the second time in January 1793. The description of the Tasmanian aborigines given by D'Entrecasteaux contrasts strongly with that given by his contemporaries of other indigenous populations. 'Their intentions were so peaceful,' he wrote, 'that they did not even dare to wake up the crewmen who were dozing. After exchanging gifts, they even danced together.' Yet the Tasmanians were attacked with ferocity by the newcomers, and died out completely, killed off as much by firearms as by the diseases imported by the invaders.

Mammals

The *Zaglossus*, a close relation of the echidna, is the only monotreme whose disappearance from the Australian mainland can be blamed on man. This animal was 3 feet (1 meter) long and lived on insects. Like the echidna, it had hair and spines, and a tube-shaped beak.

Gilbert's potoroo or rat-kangaroo, *Potorous gilberti*, frequented the marshes and watercourses. Its Aboriginal name was *ngil-gyte*. In hunting

Australia used to have two megapodes of the genus *Progura*, strange, very primitive birds that did not sit on their eggs but laid them in a large mass of vegetation. Decomposition provided the heat necessary for the young's development.

Zaglossus hacketti, a close relative of the echidna, was a giant monotreme whose disappearance from the Australian mainland can be blamed on man.

it, the Aborigines would clear a long track, and the women and old men shouted and beat the scrub to flush the animals out and drive them towards the cleared area, where they were immediately captured. In this way a tribe could kill an immense number in a few hours. The rat kangaroo could reach a length of 2 feet (60 centimeters) from head to tail. Only two specimens deposited in the British Museum are known, and the species has not been rediscovered since 1900. A related species, *Potorous platyops*,

or broad-faced potoroo, was already rare at the time of its discovery; Gould knew of only two specimens, collected in Western Australia. The last known capture goes back to 1908. This extinction appears to be due to the introduction of cats and foxes, and to bush fires. The first two species were not, like their smaller relatives, in the habit of digging burrows, and this seems to have hastened their extinction.

The barred bandicoot, *Perameles bougainville*, lived in the south and east of Australia. John Gould killed his first specimen in July 1839. He had pursued it over several hundred yards when it hid under a stone, and was

Gilbert's potoroo or rat-kangaroo, *Potorous gilberti*, is known only from two specimens and disappeared before 1900.

The broad-faced potoroo, *Potorous platyops*, became extinct about 1908.

The freckled dibbler, *Antechinus apicalis*, had litters of up to seven.

easily captured; it dug into the ground at great speed and in a manner like a running pig. He observed that it was also like a pig in the way its skin adhered to the meat. Roasted, the meat had a delicate flavor and made excellent eating. This was also the case with most if not all the other species of that genus. The barred bandicoot finally disappeared about 1940.

Another species, *Perameles myosurus*, fed on seeds, fruits and insects. It dug holes in the ground, swiftly and easily, and took refuge, when pursued, in hollow tree trunks. It had a litter of three or four young. Unlike

The barred bandicoot, *Perameles bougainville*, dug itself into the ground at speed and ran rather like a pig, according to John Gould.

Perameles myosurus, another bandicoot, was a remarkable digger.

EXTINCT SPECIES

The toolache, or Grey's wallaby, *Macropus greyi*, was a small species often hunted for its skin. Though it ran fast, dogs and hunters quickly drove it to extinction.

its extinct relative, it had a soft, fragile skin, difficult to peel off. It disappeared around 1910.

The pig-footed bandicoot, *Chaeropus ecaudatus*, showed an unusual adaptation of the forefeet, each having only two toes like a pig, while each hind foot had only one toe. In 1907 there were a few left in the Lake Eyre region, and the last accounts of surviving animals came from Aborigines of that area, in 1925.

The freckled dibbler, *Antechinus apicalis*, lived in Western Australia. The naturalist Gilbert noted that the female of the species bore up to seven young. A fold in the skin and extra-long body hair served as a pouch.

Grey's wallaby, *Macropus greyi*, was named for its discoverer, a famous explorer of South Australia. It was a small wallaby, measuring a little less than 3 feet (0.9 meter) long, and living in the deforested zones close to the sea or the salt lakes of Southern Australia. Gould wrote that he had never seen so fast an animal; it did not even seem to be concerned when a dog came very close to it, but when it did take off it went with a leap like an antelope, taking a short jump first, then a big one, leaving the dog standing. The skins of these wallabies sold so well that only six animals were counted in 1924. The last wild specimen known was taken and wounded by dogs trained for kangaroo hunting; it survived for 2 years. The last known specimen lived in the Adelaide Zoo, where it died about 1940.

The brown hare-wallaby, *Lagorchestes leporides*, was a small wallaby whose general behavior, hide, and even ears were reminiscent of the European hare. Gould described it as a rather solitary animal, often lying comfortably in a snug spot behind a tuft of grass on the open plains. Again, its leaping take-off was remarkable. Gould tells of an adventure he had when hunting the animal in South Australia. He was on a plain with two fast dogs, when they raised a hare-wallaby and chased it for 400 yards

The coat and ears of the brown hare-wallaby, *Lagorchestes leporides*, were very like those of the European hare, and its behavior was similar.

(nearly 400 m); suddenly it turned and came back towards him with the dogs at its heels. After a second's hesitation, it jumped straight up on to his head, and as it leapt down again he was able to shoot it, and so got his specimen. The European fox, brought in to eliminate the rabbit at the beginning of last century, was no doubt the most formidable enemy this animal met, and no more hare-wallabies were found after 1890.

The thylacine or Tasmanian wolf, *Thylacinus cynocephalus*, had a reputation as a monstrous nocturnal predator. It had very powerful jaws with which it used to crush the head of its victims. It lived on kangaroos, wallabies, and ground-nesting birds. Its reputation was worsened by its killing of sheep, or dogs that were too rash. It would not hesitate to devour animals caught in traps, so the trappers ended up setting poison baits for the thylacines. Some farmers claimed the thylacine was a sort of vampire that drank the blood of its victims. This animal at one time had lived on the mainland, withdrawing as the dingoes spread, to end up in Tasmania, an island with no other big carnivore.

From 1888 to 1914, premiums were paid by both the government and the Van Diemen's Land Company that led to the destruction of 2268 thylacines over nearly 16 years. The two last known captures took place between 1930 and 1933; the last animal of all was put in the Hobart Zoo where it died later the same year. Official protection came from the Australian Government a little late, in 1938. Expeditions in 1937–8, 1945, 1946, and then 1963, found not a single animal, but did find footprints.

A hundred years earlier Gould had predicted that when Tasmania had a larger population and its forests became dissected by roads, the numbers of thylacines would decrease rapidly and they would finally be exterminated, so joining the wolf of England and Scotland as an animal of the past. He considered this would be a great loss, but felt shepherds and farmers could not be blamed for wanting to rid the island of such a problematic creature. There was already a bounty for the head of the 'tiger,'

The Tasmanian wolf, *Thylacinus cynocephalus*, also called a 'tiger.' This animal at one time lived on mainland Australia but withdrew as the dingoes spread, finally ending up in Tasmania, an island with no other big carnivore. The last specimen, a young male, was killed in 1961.

as it was also called, but for some time the caves of the rocky ravines of Tasmania, covered with dense forest, would prevent its destruction.

During prehistoric times, many species of marsupial disappeared. The giant forms, the Diprodontidae, did not survive the arrival of man. The largest marsupial skull recorded measures 6 feet (2 meters). These animals

The extinct Diprodontidae family included some giant marsupials that were among the largest of Australia's extinct fauna. In appearance they often resembled rhinoceroses or hippopotamuses more than kangaroos.

Procoptodon was a kangaroo 6 feet (2 meters) tall, with only one toe on each foot.

Palorchestes, a marsupial 12 feet (3.6 meters) tall with a trunk whose behavior and diet still remain unknown. It has been described as the most unsightly animal ever exterminated by man.

were quite unusual; their incisors were like those of rabbits, their hind legs recall those of their climbing ancestors, and in general appearance they resembled the rhinoceros or the hippopotamus more than the kangaroo.

The giant marsupial *Palorchestes* is known only by fossils contemporary with man. It was nearly 12 feet (3.6 meters) tall, had a trunk, and has been described as the most unsightly animal ever exterminated by humans.

North America
From the First Indians to the Last Cowboys

North America has an area of more than 7.3 million square miles (19 million square kilometers) and was settled more than 30,000 years ago by Native Americans who crossed Bering Strait on an ice bridge, since the glaciations had solidified huge volumes of water. The present population of North America (including Canada) is more than 270 million, and the continent is well known for its prodigious economic development. Popular imagery of it includes bison, grizzly bears, and coyotes.

The Native Americans, with a population of several million in 1700, were ruthlessly harrassed by the white settlers. In 1759, for example, the commander-in-chief of the English troops, Lord Jeffrey Amherst, was accused of distributing blankets contaminated with smallpox,

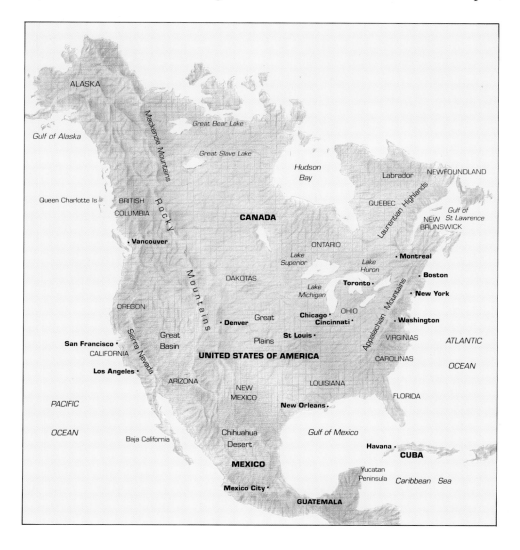

Native Americans drying fish and game over an open fire.

yellow fever, and other diseases among the Iroquoi. Cholera, measles, and chicken pox caused tens of thousands of Native American deaths, and by 1920 they numbered fewer than a quarter of a million. By 1927 there were more automobiles in the USA than there were Native Americans.

Newfoundland, included in this chapter, was inhabited by the Beothuk tribe, among others. This tall tribe was to disappear last century because of the white people.

It was on this continent, settled early, with its natural environments profoundly changed to meet the needs of grazing and agriculture, and despite the establishment of remarkable reserves, that the greatest organized slaughters of all time occurred. This happened to the bison, the passenger pigeon, and others.

North America thus holds several records for the scope of the massacres and for the elimination of 17 species and subspecies of freshwater fish.

Fish

The fat-tailed dace, *Gila crassicauda*, lived in calm watercourses and stagnant waterholes in California. It could grow to a length of 1 foot (30 centimeters), and was for long the favorite fish of the Native Americans. It was still very plentiful when the scientific world learnt of it in 1854,

North America has 17 extinct species or subspecies of freshwater fish. This one is the hare-lipped suckerfish, *Lagochilla lacera*, last caught in 1893.

but the drainage and other changes to the watercourses rapidly became too much for it. In addition, the introduction of other fish into its habitat made many hybridizations possible. The last known dace was taken about 1945, and a few hybrids are still regularly caught, but the pure race seems today to have totally disappeared.

The hare-lipped suckerfish, *Lagochilla lacera*, swarmed in the basins of the Ohio and Mississippi Rivers. Its lower lip was almost divided into two, a remarkable adaptation for grazing on the algae that grew on the pebbles and the rocky or gravelly river bottoms. With deforestation and intensive grazing and cultivation, soil erosion caused a permanent discharge of mud that made the water turbid; the algae on which the fish fed disappeared and the fish themselves were asphyxiated by the clay-laden water. The last of these suckerfish was caught in 1893.

The snub-nosed suckerfish, *Chasmistes brevirostris*, lived in Lake Klamathy, in Oregon State. It apparently reproduced in the neighbouring rivers, because although the quality of the lake's water had hardly changed, the water in the rivers was a different matter. The last one was taken in 1960.

A closely related species, Juin's suckerfish, lived in Lake Utah. A fishery was set up on the Provo River where this fish reproduced, the people living almost exclusively off the catch. From 1935 on, there were severe droughts that made the fish scarce, and the last one was caught in 1959.

Two species of cisco, *Coregonus nigripennus* and *C. johannae*, lived in the Great Lakes of Huron and Michigan. They were heavily fished, for example 15 million tons were caught in 1885. They were caught mainly with nets that caught up to 10 tons a day, but also by line during winter, reducing the fish numbers to the point where, from 1940 on, it was no longer profitable to take up cisco fishing as a trade. The last specimen was caught in 1960.

The lampreys that were introduced into the Great Lakes completed the elimination of these two species. Lampreys also exterminated the lake trout, *Salvelinus namaycush*, that in the meantime was acclimatized to some South American lakes, where it caused irreparable damage to other species but still survives.

The rare springs of the Chihuahua Desert were home to three other fish species. These springs were diverted to power mills, to establish water reservoirs into which carp were introduced, and to set up irrigation systems, thus finally destroying the native fishes' habitat. The two minnows, *Stypodon signifer* and *Dionda episcopa plunctifer*, and the cyprinodontid *Cyprinodon latifasciatus*, which lived there, disappeared about 1930.

Birds

Some bird species have disappeared from North America since the arrival of the Native Americans.

Among the birds of prey, the genus *Breagyps*, a large condor that is very plentiful in the famous La Brea tar pits of California, was extinct before the arrival of the Europeans. The painted vulture, *Sarcorhamphus sacra*, is so little known that even its very existence cannot be properly validated. It was described by the naturalist Bartram in 1791, but no specimen was ever collected. It was about the size of a turkey, but smaller than the painted vulture of Florida. Its feathers were white apart from a few wing feathers and a dark brown tail. Its red head had orange folds in the skin, and the iris was golden. In Louisiana, about 1758, the bird was so rare that the Native Americans were paying very large sums for its feathers, used as ornaments, or its bones, used in manufacturing peace pipes. It became extinct during the 19th century.

The Labrador duck, *Camptorhynchus labradorius*, frequented the east coast during winter, from New Brunswick to Chesapeake Bay. No one seems to have located its breeding ground during its existence, and it died

No one was able to discover the breeding grounds of the Labrador duck, *Camptorhynchus labradorius*, during its existence, and it died out about 1875.

The extinct subspecies of seaside sparrow
Ammospiza maritima.

out about 1875. Some 50 are preserved in museums round the world.

On June 17, 1987, in the Disney World park in Florida, the last specimen of a subspecies of the seaside sparrow *Ammospiza maritima*, died in its cage. This subspecies had been virtually extinct since 1980, only five males having been caught in an attempt to preserve the species. These captures seem to have been a waste of time. They would have made survival possible if a female had been among those taken.

A subspecies of prairie chicken, the heath hen *Tympanuchus cupido cupido*, lived on the plains of Massachusetts and Carolina until 1870. Two other subspecies still survive, but are so few that conservation measures have had to be taken. The name *cupido* (cupid) comes from their extraordinary courtship display. The males gather in dozens, stamping on the ground, tail erect, head down and wings spread. Orange pouches under the neck become swollen, making a dull boom.

The first measures of protection were taken as early as 1791, when it was realized that the bird was endangered; the aim was to ban hunting at certain times of the year, but this was unsuccessful. Some people saw no more reason to protect 'woodcocks' than Native Americans. At the same time, the birds were so plentiful that servants had to ask their masters not to serve them up more than a few times a week. The arrival around 1800 of cats, rats and dogs, and the conversion of large tracts of grassland to arable farms, caused a rapid decline in numbers. The introduction of

A subspecies of the prairie chicken, the heath hen, *Tympanuchus cupido cupido*. The last bird died at the age of 8 in 1932 in a reserve on the island of Martha's Vineyard, where it had nearly been run over several times.

pheasants and other poultry led to the appearance of new diseases that
contributed to the growing scarcity, so that by 1870 the bird had disappeared from the continent and survived only on a few islands.

Its last refuge was the island of Martha's Vineyard, where it survived
until 1932. In 1890 there were only 200 there, in 1896 about 100, and
in 1908, when a reserve was set up, about 60. The success of the reserve,
with 20,000 birds recorded in 1915, was largely offset by poachers, who
left many traces of their presence. At the beginning of 1917, as a result

Hundreds of millions of passenger pigeons,
Ectopistes migratorius, were slaughtered
by humans last century. The young birds
were the most prized and hunters did not
hesitate to chop down trees to get them
after the massive flocks settled.

of a fire in 1916, the multiplication that year of a species of goshawk, and a hard winter, there were only 150 left. In 1925 the cats on the island — more than 100 of them — were exterminated. This fall in the number of predators was paralleled by a drop to about 20 birds by the end of the year, the poachers having continued their work despite the few targets they had. In 1928 there were 13 left, in 1929 only two could be found. From 1930 on the last prairie chicken in the reserve was its major attraction. By sheer luck this old male avoided more than once being run over by cars, and it died, aged 8, in March 1932.

One of the most incredible stories in the history of extinctions is certainly that of the passenger pigeon, *Ectopistes migratorius*. The Native Americans had been hunting it for thousands of years before the appearance of the Europeans, who slaughtered the bird in huge numbers for eating and for fattening pigs. The pigeons nested in gigantic flocks that some naturalists occasionally tried to count. Wilson in 1910 estimated one single flock to contain 2,230,272,000 birds. According to figures quoted by John Audubon, the famous American ornithologist, the food intake of such a flock was nearly a million tons a day, an indication of how rapidly crops and forests could be devastated. To find food, the pigeons had to travel regularly, sometimes well over 100 miles (161 kilometers) a day. During a stay on the banks of the Ohio in 1913, Audubon wrote in astonished tones of the abundance of these birds:

As the time of the arrival of the passenger pigeons approached, their foes anxiously prepared to receive them. Some persons were ready with iron pots containing sulphur, others with torches of pine knots; many had poles, and the rest, guns . . . Everything was ready and all eyes were fixed on the clear sky that could be glimpsed amid the tall tree-tops . . . Suddenly a general cry burst forth, 'Here they come!' The noise they made, even though still distant, reminded me of a hard gale at sea, passing through the rigging of a close-reefed vessel. As the birds arrived and passed over me, I felt a current of air that surprised me. Thousands of the pigeons were soon knocked down by the polemen, whilst more continued to pour in. The fires were lighted, then a magnificent, wonderful, almost terrifying sight presented itself. The pigeons, arriving by the thousands, alighted everywhere, one above another, until solid masses were formed on the branches all around. Here and there the perches gave way with a crack under the weight, and fell to the ground, destroying hundreds of birds beneath, and forcing down the dense groups of them with which every stick was loaded. The scene was one of uproar and confusion. I found it quite useless to speak or even to shout, to those persons nearest to me. Even the gun reports were seldom heard, and I was made aware of the firing only by seeing the shooters reloading.

No one dared venture nearer the devastation. Meanwhile, the hogs had been penned up. The picking up of the dead and wounded birds was put off till morning. The pigeons were constantly coming, and it was past midnight before I noticed any decrease in the number of those arriving. The uproar continued the whole night. I was anxious to know how far this sound could be heard, so I sent off a man used to roaming the forest, who returned in two hours with the information that he had heard it distinctly three

The ivory-billed
woodpecker *Campephilus
principalis*, as painted by
Audubon. Its beak was
particularly prized by the
Indians, who used it to
make crowns for their
chiefs and braves. Hunting
and the destruction of its
habitat by logging caused
the extinction of the
species by 1962.

The last Carolina parrot, *Conuropsis carolinensis*, survived in the zoo at Cincinnati until September 1, 1914. It was in the same zoo and same year that the last passenger pigeon also died.

miles [five kilometers] from the roosting place.

Towards the approach of day, the noise somewhat subsided. Long before I could distinguish them plainly, the pigeons began to move off in a direction quite different from the one in which they flew when they arrived in the evening before. By sunrise all that were able to fly had disappeared. The howling of the wolves now reached our ears, and the foxes, the lynxes, cougars, bears, racoons, opossums and polecats were sneaking off. Eagles and hawks, accompanied by a crowd of vultures, took their place and enjoyed their share of the spoils. Then the author of all this devastation began to move among the dead, the dying and the mangled, picking up the pigeons and piling them in heaps. When each man had as many as he could possibly dispose of, the hogs were let loose to feed on the remainder. The young pigeons were the most prized, and hunters did not hesitate to cut down trees to get them.

In New York in 1805, the price per bird was 1 cent; in 1830, at the same markets, it was already 4 cents. By about 1870, the birds were reproducing only in the Great Lakes region. Some small flights of birds were observed in 1880. When a flock of 250,000 was seen in 1896, a mob of hunters, alerted by telegraph, came to meet them, and probably fewer than 10,000 of the birds survived. The last wild specimen was sighted in 1899. A reward of $1500 was offered in 1909 to anyone who could provide evidence of nest-building by a pair, but the money never had to be paid out. The last bird died in the Cincinnati Zoo on September 1, 1914.

In the same zoo, and in the same year, the last representative of the Carolina parrot, *Conuropsis carolinensis*, was also to die. There were in fact two distinct subspecies, whose numbers must have been considerable according to the hunters' accounts. These parrots were reputed to be harmful to crops. They loved seeds and fruits and naturally frequented the flower and vegetable gardens, where they were systematically destroyed. Hunters also considered them interesting game. They were much appreciated as aviary birds, and thousands were privately owned. Unfortunately they never reproduced in captivity, and the last specimen was caught in 1901. This species lived in the southeastern United States, and although it was exterminated by humans, it seems possible that disease may also have played a part in its disappearance.

The ivory-billed woodpecker, *Campephilus principalis*, was very common in the United States until 1930, and the last five birds were observed in 1962. It frequented the dense forest, not far from watercourses. Hunting, and bringing these areas into cultivation and draining them, caused its extinction. It nested in dead trees in riverside forests, so logging deprived it of suitable habitat. This was a big woodpecker, reaching 20 inches (51 centimeters), and the territory of each pair covered up to 1900 acres (800 hectares). Its beak was particularly prized by the Native Americans, who used it to make crowns for their chiefs and brave warriors. When the bird became rare, the Native Americans had no hesitation in exchanging specimens for two deerskins each. The survival of the Cuban subspecies is seriously endangered today; the few that remain cannot be expected to last longer than a few decades.

Two of the four subspecies of bison have disappeared from North America; this is the Pennsylvanian bison.

Mammals

One of the American army's objectives was to eliminate the Native Americans, and one of its methods was to get rid of the animals they depended on for food. The American bison, *Bison bison*, was the basic resource of the Native American economy, industry and food. They ate the meat, the skins clothed them and served as a roof, the bones were used to make tools, knives, needles, hooks, and children's toys; and the horns and hooves were fashioned into kitchen utensils. So the bison became the army's target, and this contributed to the near-extinction of the species. It must be pointed out, however, that the Native Americans too joined in the slaughter and were very wasteful of the bison as a resource. When the Europeans arrived, the total American bison population was estimated at 75 million. Bison hunting from 1720 to 1830 satisfied the needs of leather production and the bringing of new land under the plough. During the 1870s, 2.5 million bison were killed annually over the whole continent. Since old bulls could weigh up to 2600 pounds (1200 kilograms), we are compelled to estimate an annual kill of more than 2 million tons.

William Frederick Cody, better known as Buffalo Bill, won fame by killing 4280 bison in 18 months to feed the workers building the railway. The bison skins were left on the spot, then picked up again when they were clean, and turned into fertilizer or animal-black. The Santa Fe railroad in the 1870s transported 25,000 tons of bison bones. Thirty years earlier, it had taken 3 days to traverse a herd of bison covering an estimated area of 1350 square miles (3500 square kilometers). The American Bison Society was founded in 1905 for the purpose of preserving what could still be saved.

Of the four American subspecies, only two survive today. The eastern bison, *Bison bison pennsylvanicus*, and the Oregon bison, *B. b. oreganus*, have died out. In 1790, there was only one herd of eastern bison in Pennsylvania — an estimated 300–400 animals. It was greatly reduced by the harsh winter of 1799–1800. The last survivor, a male, was killed in

---

Wolves

Eight North American subspecies of wolves are today extinct, because of the way they were intensively hunted. From 1850 on, poisoning was done instead of hunting. Strychnine was the poison most used, being remarkably effective for all its disadvantages. (It also killed cattle, for example, and claimed several humans.) From 1850 to 1900, two million wolves were killed.

The biggest of the North American wolves, *Canis lupus alces*, inhabited the Kenai Peninsula in Alaska, no doubt hunting the elk. It was exterminated in 1915.

The black wolf of Florida, *Canis rufus floridanus*, disappeared in 1917.

The Texas gray wolf, *Canis lupus monstrabilis*, disappeared in 1920, at the same time as the New Mexico wolf.

The lobo, *Canis lupus nubilus*, disappeared in 1926 after being for a long time the most common wolf in North America. It lived in Manitoba and southern Texas.

The Southern Rockies wolf, *Canis lupus youngi*, lived in the states of Nevada, Colorado, and Utah. It disappeared about 1940.

Another subspecies living in the Cascade Range in British Columbia, *Canis lupus fuscus*, disappeared in 1950.

The Texas red wolf, *Canis rufus rufus*, (illustrated right), disappeared in 1970.

Remains of *Canis dirus*, the dire wolf, and the smaller *C. orcutti* occur in the famous La Brea tar pits of California.

1802. The eastern bison became extinct in 1825, when a cow and its calf were killed by hunters at Valley Head in West Virginia.

The Mexican grizzly, *Ursus arctos nelsoni*, was impressive in stature, attaining a length of more than 6 feet (2 meters), and weight of up to 660 pounds (300 kilograms), even though it was the smallest of the North American bears. The type specimen was killed at Chihuahua in 1899, although the species had been known to European explorers since the 1500s. In 1960, only 30 were counted in a census, and during the four following years graziers continued to poison or trap the bears, so that none survived after 1964.

The North American jaguar, *Felis onca*, that had a much-prized skin, disappeared from North America in 1905, while the South American species continues to be hunted.

The Queen Charlotte Islands caribou, *Rangifer tarandus dawsoni*, inhabited Queen Charlotte Island in British Columbia (Canada). The Haida Indians, who had been on the island for several thousand years, had no knowledge of the caribou's existence, because it frequented only the inland areas. When the trade in skins took off with the arrival of the Europeans, Native Americans who brought in caribou skins were rewarded with a bonus. First mention of this species goes back to 1880, but there was no scientific description of it until 1900. It was already on the verge of extinction, because several hunting campaigns were unsuccessful for lack of game.

The Dawson caribou of Queen Charlotte Island, *Rangifer tarandus dawsoni*, was a victim of the fur trade.

However, in November 1908, two males and a female with a kid were observed. The three adults were killed, and only the young one survived because it had not dared approach as close as its unfortunate companions had.

There were two subspecies of elk, one living in Canada, the other in the American states of New Mexico and Arizona. *Cervus canadensis canadensis*, of eastern Canada, died out about 1840. It had provided meat and leather for the many Native American tribes of the great northern plains, almost as much as the bison. The most prized parts were the upper canines, used as ornaments by the Native American women. The white Brotherhood of the Elks organized tremendous drives to get the canine teeth with which they made chains for their watches, symbols of the Brotherhood. As the elks became scarce, the Arizona subspecies, *Cervus canadensis merriami*, was hunted down in its turn. It was still flourishing when the Canadian form disappeared, since herds of more than 2000 were fairly frequently observed. Measures to protect the elk were instituted from 1870 on, but the hunt continued in this part of the USA, where the ranches and the fences tolerated only cattle. The last Arizona elk were killed in 1906 in the Chiricahara mountains. Their extinction may seem surprising in view of the animal's wide distribution in the past, and the many refuges it had been able to find in the mountains above 10,000 feet (9800 meters).

The North American mastodon was much hunted by the Native Americans.

The Badlands (or Audubon's) bighorn sheep, *Ovis canadensis auduboni*, had disappeared by the 1920s, and possibly as early as 1905. After finding refuge on rocky promontories in the Dakotas, the sheep were isolated

there, hunted by dogs, and killed. This was a sheep of impressive stature, weighing up to 330 pounds (150 kilograms). Like its Rocky Mountains relative, it was timorous but very agile on the steep cliffs where it found refuge.

The sea mink, *Mustela macrodon*, lived in the coastal regions of New England and Canada. It was not only longer than its relatives, measuring 32 inches (81 centimeters), but also broader and fatter. It was easily twice the length and weight of the continental form. The Native Americans hunted it for its skin and meat. The trappers found it easier to hunt, and its fur, more russet than that of the inland form, was especially appreciated. A victim of the fur trade, the last specimen was killed in 1880 and its skin sold.

Long before Christopher Columbus arrived, several species of big mammals had disappeared. Examples are the North American mammoth; the giant beaver, *Casteroides*, that was 6 feet (nearly 2 meters) long; the western camel, *Camelops hesternus*; and a lion, *Panthera leo atrox* that no doubt was hunted by the Native Americans. The mammoth, like its European counterpart, was also hunted over its vast territory by the Native Americans. These extinctions are therefore not only from the effect of firearms, even if North America was subsequently the location of the most staggering massacres ever organized.

A giant beaver, more than 6 feet (2 meters) long, also was probably hunted out by the Native Americans.

South America
A Hidden Fauna

Human settlement of South America is relatively recent, going back only about 10,000 years. The Native Americans, who were of North American origin, crossed the Isthmus of Panama to come south. The civilizations that developed, of the Mayas and the Incas, were on the same scale as their continent.

Deforestation is like an open wound on this continent, already creating real deserts. In the district of São Paulo alone, the forest area has been

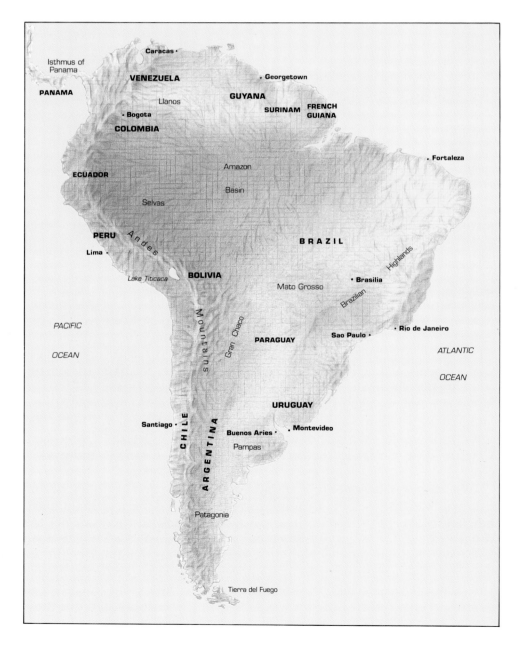

reduced by 53,000 square miles (137,500 square kilometers) since 1907, falling from 58 percent to 3 percent of the total area.

Hundreds of species are today endangered by the destruction of their habitat as well as by hunting. The chinchilla, *Chinchilla laniger*, still wild at the beginning of this century, was eliminated from its natural habitat in less than 20 years. Chinchilla farms have now appeared, ensuring the survival and the profitability of the animal. Hundreds of thousands of them were still being killed about 1900, but only 27,826 skins were officially traded in 1909. Some relict groups survive in northern Chile. If steps to farm them had not been quickly taken — and they were largely inspired by profit — the species would in all probability have disappeared.

Many monkeys are hunted by the Native Americans for their meat, as well as by 'farmers' or professional collectors who are rarely mindful of international legislation such as the Washington Convention. They figure among the world priorities of the WWF and the IUCN.

The uakari or bald-headed monkey, *Cacajao melanocephalus*, and the golden lion tamarin, *Leontideus rosalia*, as well as the Chaco wolf, the Amazonian manatee, the spectacled bear, the pampas deer, the lamas and vicuñas, which are better known to the person in the street, cannot survive long without measures of protection.

Fish

Lake Titicaca, on the frontier between Peru and Bolivia at an altitude of 12,505 feet (3812 meters), used to have a unique fish, *Orestias cuvieri*, with a flat head crowned by two large eyes. Capable of reaching a length of 12

The discovery of South America.

This flat-headed fish, *Orestias cuvieri*, endemic to Lake Titicaca, died out soon after the introduction of trout from the North American Great Lakes.

inches (30 centimeters), this fish was a major source of food for the lake-side dwellers. In 1937, 100 years after the scientific discovery of this fish, the North American Great Lakes trout, *Salvelinus namaycush*, was introduced, and this predator rapidly eliminated the local fish, the last of which were caught during World War II. There have been many attempts since then to rediscover this species but they have been fruitless. The trout was itself destroyed in its original habitat by introduced lampreys.

Birds

The only extinct tinamou, *Crypturellus saltuarius*, was described in 1950; it is known from a single specimen collected in Colombia in 1943.

The tiger heron, *Tigrisoma fasciatus fasciatus*, belongs to an endemic Brazilian subspecies. The last specimen was collected in 1912.

The pallid falcon, *Falco kreyenborgi*, endemic to Tierra del Fuego and described in 1929, is known only from five birds. It was last collected in 1961.

A subspecies of the yellow-billed pintail duck, *Anas georgica niceforoi*, disappeared in 1952.

Finally, a curassow, *Crax fasciolata pinima*, was described by von Penzeln in 1869. Eight specimens were collected in Brazil, and the bird disappeared in 1952.

Mammals

The human presence in South American is sufficiently ancient that many species, including the biggest, were already extinct when the first naturalists came to study the fauna. Only bones, thousands of years old, have come down from those species. One of the famous paleontologists, who made some of the most important paleontological discoveries in this part of the world, was Ameghino. In 1875, he discovered substantial human remains near Buenos Aires:

> I found some mixed with a large quantity of charcoal, baked earth, burnt and scored bones, arrowheads, silex chisels and knives, and a large number of our extinct animals with scoremarks and cuts clearly made by human hand.

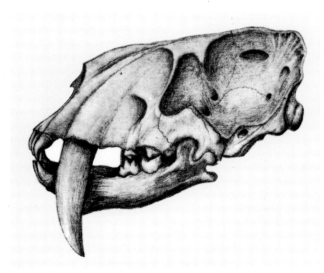

The South American fauna had many edentate mammals, like this *Megatherium*.

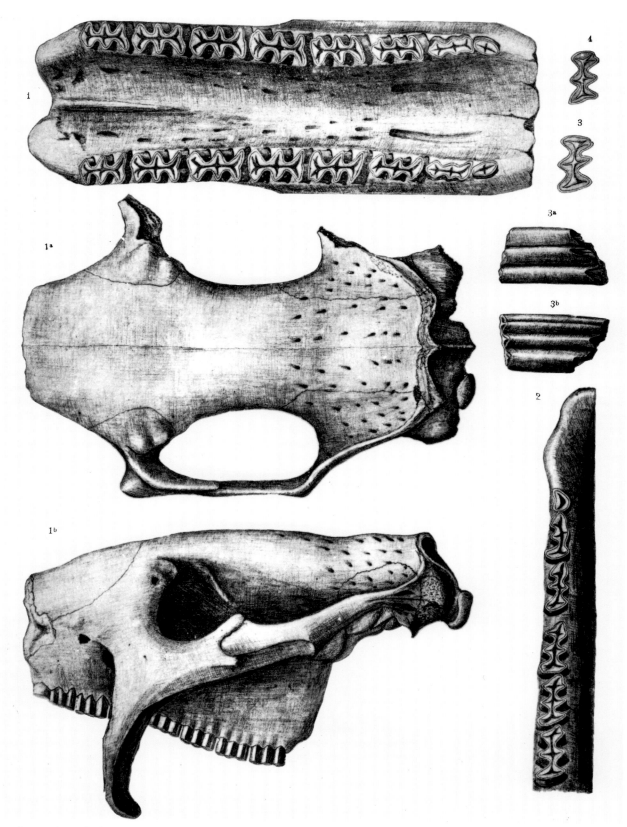

Fossil remains of giant edentate mammals.

Later, Ameghino discovered the actual dwelling of this primitive American, whose rather unusual shelter was a giant armadillo shell. Continuing his excavations, he discovered that after laying the shell on its side, the primitive human had dug out the soil round it and made himself a proper lair in which he could find temporary shelter. The shells of these animals could reach a size of nearly 6 by 5 feet (2 by 1.5 meters), and a height of more than 3 feet (1 meter).

In the province of Minas Gerais, famous today for its minerals and giant crystals, human bones were discovered in association with hundreds of animal bones belonging to at least 44 species that are now extinct. Among them were two giant edentate mammals, *Mylodon robustus* and *Taxodon platensis*; the giant armadillo, *Glyptodon elegans*; the mastodon, *Mastodon humboldtii*; the Pampas ox, *Bos pampaeus*; a bear, *Ursus bonariensis*; and a horse, *Equus neogaeus*.

Most large species had disappeared before the arrival of the Europeans, but today many others are extinct or seriously endangered. Fortunately, South America is a vast continent, and many refuge zones still exist, the preservation of which is imperative.

Glyptodon, a giant armadillo, was hunted by the Indians, who used its shell as a shelter. Some shells grew to 6 x 5 feet (2 x 1.5 meters) and reached a height of more than 3 feet (1 meter).

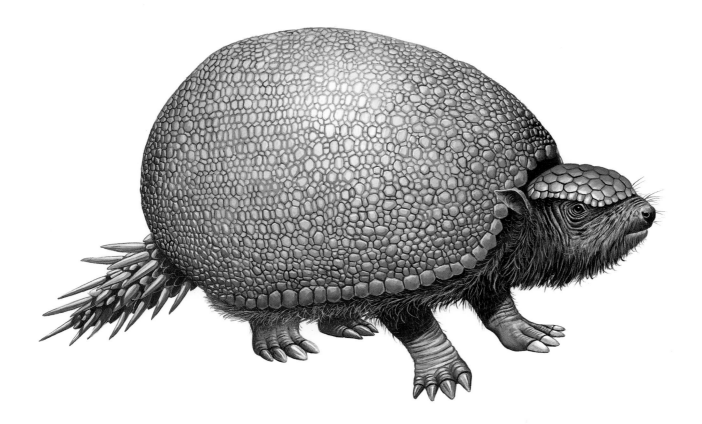

Tomorrow

These stories of extinct animals, which all have to be told in the past tense, could in the very near future be the subject of an encyclopedia of several volumes. The private American research institute World Watch, specializing in environmental problems, has just published an impressive report. It foresees by the year 2000 the disappearance of one-fifth of the species at present living on Earth, and considers that the rate of extinction of animal and plant species could by the end of the century be several hundred per day.

The extinction of species has become an issue in the news, and the media have recently become interested in the fate of the most endangered animals. International organizations such as the International Union for Conservation of Nature, the World Wildlife Fund and others are making tremendous efforts to safeguard hundreds of species. Their actions have already made it possible to put several dozen out of danger, but the future of the majority remains uncertain. At a time when we can control bacteria and have mastery of the atom, develop clones of carrots and mice, walk on the moon and place instruments on Mars, know the exchange rate of the dollar in Paris, Tokyo, and Los Angeles all at the same moment, we are still often powerless to preserve a species.

The panda, *Ailuropoda melanoleuca*, emblem of the WWF and symbol of the protection of Nature, could disappear before the middle of next century in spite of our efforts. Its rarity, the difficulty of observing it scientifically in the wild, the increasing number of cases of sterility and deaths from starvation, lead us to fear the worst. At least, that is the conclusion

New Caledonia's emblem, the kagu, *Rhynochetus jubatus*, has top world priority with the International Council for the Protection of Birds.

reached by participants of an international colloquium for the protection of species, held in 1987.

The kagu, *Rhynochetus jubatus*, endemic to New Caledonia, belongs to a unique and endangered family of birds. Its numbers are thought to be down to about 1000, living in remote forested areas of the mountains. It is considered top priority by the International Council for the Protec-

According to many international experts, the panda, *Ailuropoda melanoleuca*, is doomed to early extinction.

tion of Birds. The kagu is still not well known to ornithologists, and the means of protection are very underfunded. Yet the finances needed for preliminary study and conservation measures, so difficult to obtain, are no more than the price of a dozen stuffed specimens.

Among the endangered plant species, some have almost died out. This is the case with the dodo tree, for example, and the New Caledonian palm *Pritchardiopsis jeanneneyi*, whose heart was so appreciated by the convicts. There was only one adult tree left when a horticultural scheme was started to save the species.

The causes of disappearance are many and overlap one another. Hunting, as we have seen, is one of the main factors, and the last 200 years have witnessed rapid development of hunting and fishing as industries. Financial interests, too, have grown, clashing more and more with those of the wild world. Hunting of sea mammals, whales and seals, is the supreme conflict of financial interests with Nature, and has almost extinguished several marine species. Although at present many countries have given up hunting or trading in marine mammals, more than 40 factory ships continue to butcher whales for processing into canned pet food and the raw materials for lipstick.

Our knowledge of the extreme difficulties faced by the wild world no longer allows us to remain indifferent.

Pollution also seriously threatens our environment and ourselves. Oil spills have left the public with the memory of oiled birds and long tracts

The New Caledonian palm, *Pritchardiopsis jeanneneyi*, survives as only one adult plant, but should be saved from extinction by the cultivation of seedlings.

Each year oil spills destroy several hundred thousand birds, when so little effort would be needed to prevent this.

Apart from being lost through illegal poaching, entire herds of elephants 'have' to be killed to protect cultivated land and preserve grazing for cattle.

of polluted coastline. Because of the archaic international maritime code, oil companies owning tankers that have broken up on some coasts have sometimes preferred to lose ship and cargo rather than share their value with possible salvagers. However, tanker accidents are actually the source of less than 5 percent of the oil lost in the world's oceans; the rest comes from the flushing out of tanks that is done at sea because there are then no port dues to pay.

Other accidents such as those involving dioxin at Seveso, the Union Carbide disaster at Bhopal, and the discharge into the Rhine from the Sandoz factory at Basel, Switzerland, are well known to the public because they seriously affected the environment and caused losses of human life. Arising from negligence or human error, these events show clearly that we are always at risk from accidents, and that no safety measure can be regarded as unnecessary, however much it costs.

The effects of other forms of pollution, such as acid rain or heavy metals, are much more lasting and go much deeper. To show only limited concern for them in the meantime is to make a mistake that will have to be paid for later.

It seems that measures controlling pollution are only looked into when the most serious accidents occur. The Minamata affair in Japan had to precede a check on outflows of mercury; and the Amoco Cadiz accident in the North Sea had to precede stricter control of maritime trade.

Nuclear power and weapons testing, which some still dare to proclaim innocuous, have been the subject of all sorts of misinformation and deception, among the worst that politicians or the interested parties have ever invented. Chernobyl is not the only nuclear accident recorded, even though

Hunting the whales still goes on, even though many countries have forbidden trade in whale products.

it was the most deadly. In the name of whose interests has the truth been hidden?

Behind the arms race, the nuclear and chemical industries, looms the grave problem of what happens to their wastes. A few milligrams of benzo-3,4-pyrene are enough to cause cancer, yet hundreds of tons of it are cast into the sea even though it is known not to be biodegradable. And the halflife of nuclear waste can be more than a billion years.

Seveso's dioxin, Mururoa's radioactive clouds, and the lead in our exhausts, are in the air that we breathe and that our children will breathe. The rain takes them into the watercourses that also are polluted by fertilizers and detergents. Must we continue to discard and pollute without worrying about the environment of tomorrow?

Humans are responsible for Nature and for living creatures. The facts are there. Let each one judge, and perhaps take action.

The control of pollution depends on a general awareness; on drastic measures; on permanent, total checking procedures — objectives that it seems impossible to attain today. Because human demography and the destruction of environments are constantly growing, it is to be feared that in the time of our children and grandchildren, the wildernesses will be totally remote from their homes. Catching a fish in the river, seeing a tern or a green woodpecker, or even a patch of native forest, stands the chance of being a rarity by the year 2050.

Thanks to genetic engineering, it is uncertain whether future generations will be able to see bulls and rams, because their sperm alone will satisfy needs. The surviving species will certainly be the ones already

The accident at the Sandoz factory in Basel, Switzerland. Pollution is a contemporary plague whose consequences for our environment are sometimes difficult to judge, but that has some immediately measurable effects.

In 2028 the world population will be ten billion; if we continue to pollute the world like this, what will they eat?

known, which have proved their great adaptability to the human environment, together with the rats, cockroaches, sparrows, pigeons, etc., as well as the species man gets profit from (cows, sheep, etc.) or whose company he appreciates (cats, dogs). Just as it is no longer possible to observe the Przewalski horses outside a zoo, so our children and grandchildren will no doubt miss out on seeing elephants, pandas, rhinoceroses, and other large mammals except at the cinema or in museum galleries.

Is this progress?

To rediscover these species, naturalists will have to spend much time in the wild, searching in the most remote corners. They will question the locals, and look for traces of survivors. Some of this research will take months, or years, and one day find success.

The steps taken by the world bodies charged with the protection of nature generally provide as immediate protection of the habitats as possible. When justified, introduced predators will be tracked and their numbers limited as far as possible. Hunting and even entry to the habitat area will be checked and supervised. The rarity of a species can arouse the most covetous desires, so any trade will also be subject to supervision. Research in the wild is often also necessary for a better understanding of the biology and requirements of the species, and the dangers threatening it. If the numbers and the biology of the species allow it, and if the habitat has suffered excessive modification, reproduction in captivity will then be tried.

Chernobyl proved the potential danger of nuclear energy: in the wake of this accident were many lies, secrets, vested interests — and much damage.

None of these actions will be effective without the understanding of the wider public, and the contribution of the authorities, nor without the necessary financial means.

A gigantic experimental Noah's Ark scheme has just been launched in the United States. It should make it possible to test the survival of animal and plant species as well as a human couple, placed in complete autarky for two years.

The annual budget for world armament is a thousand billion dollars. The budget for the conservation of Nature is no more than half a billion dollars, a mere two-thousandth of that amount. It is all a question of means, and of choice — even for the environment.

Protect or destroy: we cannot delay choosing.

Demography and the Survival of Species

The growth of the human population of the world, at present 5 billion and expected to reach 10 billion by the year 2028, will necessitate more intensive exploitation of natural resources. Biologists and ecologists, as well as politicians and economists, are beginning to express concern about the consequences of this overpopulation.

The use of the natural resources produced by our planet is at stake today. The net primary production of Earth (including the oceans) is some 225 billion tons a year. According to some experts, humans today directly use, or divert or reduce totally, nearly 60 percent of the annual production. This leaves only 40 percent for all the other living species.

Conversion to desert, pollution, breaking in for pasture or cultivation, all of which are increasing, will continue to reduce this smaller share. As for the increase in the human population, it is a sombre omen for the coming years.

Dying forests all over the world warn of the growing environmental crisis.

PLANTS AND ANIMALS THAT HUMANS HAVE MADE EXTINCT

NOTE: + indicates the species became extinct shortly after the date shown.

PLANTS

Hibiscadelphus bombycinas	Hawaii	1912
Hibiscadelphus wilderianus	Hawaii	c.1950
Santalum fernandezianum	Juan Fernandez Islands	1916
Viola cryana	France	1950
Pseudophœnyx ekmanii	Santo Domingo	1926
Streblorrhyza leguminosa	Norfolk Island	1912
Trochetia erythroxylon	Canary Islands	

INVERTEBRATES

Several hundred invertebrate species have disappeared. This is particularly true of land snails, and most of all the species that lived on islands. For example, destruction of virgin forests of the Pacific Islands has caused the disappearance of more than 100 species.

FISHES

TELEOSTS

Catostomatidae

Lagochila lacera	North America	1893
Chasmistes brevirostris	North America	1960
Chasmistes liorus	North America	1959
Pantosteus sp.	North America	c.1950

Coregonidae

Coregonus nigripennus	Lakes Michigan and Huron	1960
Coregonus johannae	Lakes Michigan and Huron	1960

Cottidae

Cottus echinatus	North America	1959

Cyprinidae

Gila crassicauda	North America	1854
Stypodon signifer	North America	1930
Dionda episcopa plunctifer	North America	1930
Lepidomeda mollispinis pratensis	North America	1950
Lepidomeda altivelis	North America	1950
Rhynichtys osculus reliquus	North America	1950

Cyprinodontidae

Orestias cuvieri	South America (Lake Titicaca)	1950
Cyprinodon latifasciatus	North America	1930
Cyprinodon nevadensis calidae	North America	1960
Empetrichtys merriami	North America	1948
Empetrichtys latops pahrump	North America	1950
Empetrichtys latops concavus	North America	1950

Protroctidae

Prototroctes oxyrhinchus	New Zealand	1923

AMPHIBIANS

ANEURA

Ranidae

Rana pipiens fisheri	North America	1966

Discoglossidae

Discoglossus nigriventer	Lake Hula (Syria/Israel)	1956

REPTILES

TURTLES

Meiolaniidae

Meiolania platyceps	New Caledonia	200+
Meiolania sp.	New Caledonia	200+

Testudinidae

Cylindraspis vosmaeri	Indian Ocean (Rodriguez Island)	1800+
Cylindraspis peltastes	Indian Ocean	c.1800
Cylindraspis borbonica	Reunion Island	c.1800
Cylindraspis inepta	Maurice Island	c.1700
Cylindraspis trisserata	Maurice Island	c.1700
Cylindraspis indica	Reunion Island	1760
Cylindraspis sumeirei	Seychelles Islands	1918
Geochelone elephantopus	Galapagos Islands	1890
Geochelone abingdoni	Galapagos Islands	1876
Geochelone phantastica	Galapagos Islands	1906

CROCODILES

Mekosuchidae

Mekosuchus inexpectatus	New Caledonia	200+

Crocodylidae

Quinkana magnirostris	Australia	Holocene

LIZARDS

Geckonidae

Phelsuma edwardnewtonii	Rodriguez Island	1920
Phelsuma gigas	Rodriguez Island	1841

Scincidae

Gonglyomorphus boerii borbonica	Reunion Island	1880
Didosaurus mauritianus	Maurice Island	1650
Macroscinsus coctei	Cape Verde Islands	1940

Lacertidae

Podarcis lifordi rodriquezi	Rodriguez Island	1950

Podarcis sicula	San Stefano	
sanctistephanus	Island, Italy	1965
Iguanidae		
Cyclura collei	Jamaica	1968
Cyclura cornuta onchiopsis	Caribbean	1966
Leiocephalus eremitus	Caribbean	c.1900
Leiocephalus herminieri	Martinique	1837
Varanidae		
Megalania prisca	Australia	Holocene

SNAKES

Teidae		
Ameiva major	Martinique	1960
Ameiva cineracea	Guadeloupe	
	Island	1920
Anguidae		
Diploglossus occiduus	Jamaica	c.1880
Colubridae		
Alsophis ater	Jamaica	1960
Alsophis sancticrucis	Caribbean	
	(St Croix	
	Island)	1950
Dromicus cursor	Martinique	1962
Dromicus ornatus	Caribbean	1973
Boidae		
Bolyera multocarinata	Réunion (Ronde	
	Island)	1980

BIRDS

AEPYORNITHIFORMES		
Aepyornithidae		
Aepyornis intermedius	Madagascar	c.1600
Aepyornis maximus	Madagascar	c.1649
Aepyornis minimus	Madagascar	c.1600
Mullerornis betsilei	Madagascar	c.1600
STRUTHIONIFORMES		
Struthionidae		
Struthio asiaticus	China	c.1000
		B.C.
Struthio camelus syriacus	Near East	1966
CASUARIFORMES		
Dromaidae		
Dromaius ater	King Island	c.1850
Dromaius baudinianus	Kangaroo Island	1830
DINORNITHIFORMES		
Dinornithidae		
Dinornis maximus	New Zealand	500+
Dinornis robustus	New Zealand	500+
Dinornis torosus	New Zealand	500+
Pachyornis elephantopus	New Zealand	500+
Pachyornis mappini	New Zealand	500+
Pachyornis septentrionalis	New Zealand	600+
Emeidae		
Anomalopteryx didiformis	New Zealand	500+
Anomalopteryx oweni	New Zealand	500+

Anomalopteryx parvus	New Zealand	500+
Emeus huttoni	New Zealand	500+
Euryapteryx geranoides	New Zealand	500+
Euryapteryx gravis	New Zealand	500+
Megalapteryx benhami	New Zealand	500+
Megalapteryx didinus	New Zealand	500+
Megalapteryx hectori	New Zealand	500+
DROMORNITHIFORMES		
Dromornithidae		
Genyornis	Australia	Holocene
TINAMIFORMES		
Tinamidae		
Crypturellus saltuarius	Colombia	1943
PROCELLARIIFORMES		
Procellariidae		
Pterodroma hasitata	Caribbean	1880
carribaea		
Pterodroma rostrata becki	Solomon Islands	1928
Hydrobatidae		
Oceanodroma macrodactyla	Guadeloupe	
	Island	1912
PELECANIFORMES		
Phalacrocoracidae		
Phalacrocorax perspicillatus	Bering Islands	1852
CICONIIFORMES		
Ardeidae		
Ardea bennuides	Oman	Neolithic
Butorides mauritanicus	Maurice Island	c.1700
Nycticorax caledonicus		
crassirostris	Bonin Islands	1889
Nycticorax megacephalus	Rodriguez Island	1730
Tigrisoma fasciatum		
fasciatum	Brazil	1912
Threskiornithidae		
Apteribis	Hawaii	Holocene
Xenicibis	Jamaica	Holocene
Lampribis olivacea rotschildi	Principe Island	1901
ANSERIFORMES		
Anatidae		
Anas georgica niceforoi	South America	1952
Anas gibberifrons remissa	Rennell Island	1959
Anas oustaletti	Marianas Islands	1900+
Anas strepera couesi	Washington	
	Island	1874
Camptorhynchus labradorius	North America	1875
Cnemornis calcitrans	New Zealand	500+
Cygnus summerensis	Chatham Islands	500+
Mergus australis	Auckland Islands	1905
Rhodonessa caryophyllacea	Asia	1944
Tadorna cristata	Korea	1943
FALCONIFORMES		
Cathartidae		
Sarcorhamphus sacra	North America	c.1800
Accipitridae		
Antillovultur varonai	Cuba	Holocene
Aquila borrasi	Cuba	Holocene
Eutriorchis astur	Madagascar	1950

Falconidae
Polyborus lutosus — Guadeloupe Island — c.1900

GALLIFORMES
Cracidae
Crax fasciolata pinima — Brazil — 1955
Ortalis vetula deschaunseei — Caribbean — 1970

Tetraonidae
Tympanuchus cupido cupido — North Amercia — 1932

Phasianidae
Coturnix novaezealandiae — New Zealand — 1875
Ophrysia superciliosa — Himalayas — 1868

Meleagrididae
Meleagris californica — North America — Holocene

Gruiformes
Turnicidae
Turnix neocaledoniae — New Caledonia — 1930+

Gruidae
Grus primigenia — Europe — Paleolithic
Grus proavus — North America — Holocene

Rallidae
Amaurolimnas concolor concolor — Jamaica — 1890
Aphanapteryx bonasia — Maurice Island — 1675
Aphanapteryx leguati — Rodriguez Island — 1730
Aphanapteryx monasa — Kusaie Island — 1828
Atlantisia elpenor — Ascension Island — 1656
Atlantisia podarces — St. Helena Island — 1502+
Capellirallus karamu — New Zealand — 500+
Crecoides osborni — North America — Paleolithic
Cyanornis coerulescens — Réunion Island — 1700+
Diaphorapteryx hawkinsi — Chatham Islands — 500+
Fulica chathamensis — Chatham Islands — 500+
Fulica newtoni — Mascarenes — 1600+
Gallinula hodgeni — New Zealand — 1600+
Gallinula nesiotis — Tristan da Cunha — 1600+
Gallirallus escaudata — Society Islands — 1800+
Gallirallus hartrei — New Zealand — 500+
Gallirallus insignis — New Zealand — 500+
Gallirallus modestus — Chatham Islands — 500+
Gallirallus philippensis macquariensis — Macquarie Island — 1880
Gallirallus ripleyi — Mangaia — Holocene
Hovacrex roberti — Madagascar — Holocene
Leguatia gigantea — Maurice and Rodriguez I — 1600+
Nesoclopeus poeciloptera — Fiji — 1965
Nesotrochis deboyii — Puerto Rico — Holocene
Nesotrochis picicapensis — Cuba — Holocene
Nesotrochis steganinos — Haiti — Holocene
Pareudiastes pacificus — Samoa — 1873
Pennula millsi — Hawaii — 1864
Pennula sandwichensis — Hawaii — 1893
Poliolimnas cinereus brevipes — Iwo Jima — 1925
Porphyrio albus — Lord Howe Island — 1834
Porphyrio kukwiedei — New Caledonia — c.1750
Porphyrio mantelli hochstetteri — New Zealand — 500+

Porzana astrictocarpus — St. Helena Island — 1502+
Porzana rua — Mangaia — Holocene
Porzanula palmeri — Laysan — 1944
Rallus dieffenbachi — Chatham Islands — 1840+
Rallus muelleri — Auckland Islands — 1800+
Rallus wakensis — Wake Island — 1945
Tricholimnas lafresnayanus — New Caledonia — 1940+

Rhynochetidae
Aptornis defossor — New Zealand — Holocene
Aptornis otidiformis — New Zealand — Holocene
Rhynochetus aurarius — New Caledonia — 200+

CHARADRIIFORMES
Scolopacidae
Coenocorypha aucklandica barrierensis — Little Barrier Island (NZ) — 1870
Pisobia cooperi — — 1833
Prosobonia leucoptera — Tahiti — 1777

ALCIFORMES
Alcidae
Alca impennis — North Atlantic — 1844

COLOMBIFORMES
Raphidae
Pezophaps solitaria — Rodriguez Island — 1780
Raphus cucculatus — Maurice Island — 1680
Raphus solitarius — Réunion Island — 1750

Columbidae
Alectroenas nitidissima — Maurice Island — 1830
Alectroenas rodericana — Rodriguez Island — 1693
Caloenas canacorum — New Caledonia — 200+
Columba duboisi — Réunion Island — 1500+
Columba inornata wetmorei — Puerto Rico — 1900+
Columba jouyi — Ryuku — 1936
Columba palumbus maderensis — Madeira — 1904
Columba versicolor — Bonin Islands — 1889
Columba vitiensis godmanae — Lord Howe Island — 1853
Ducula david — Wallis Island — 300+
Ectopistes migratorius — North America — 1914
Gallicolumba ferruginea — Vanuatu — 1774
Gallicolumba longitarsus — New Caledonia — 200+
Gallicolumba norfolciensis — Norfolk Island — 1850
Hemiphaga novaezealandiae spadicea — Norfolk Island — 1801
Microgoura meeki — Choiseul — 1904
Ptilinopus mercierii mercierii — Nuku Hiva — 1849
Ptilinopus mercierii tristrami — Hiva Hoa — 1922

PSITTACIFORMES
Psittacidae
Amazona violacea — Guadeloupe Island — 1742
Amazona vittata gracilipes — Puerto Rico — 1899
Anadorhynchus glaucus — Brazil — 1950
Anadorhynchus martinicus — Martinique — 1640+
Anadorhynchus purparescens — Guadeloupe Island — 1600+
Ara atwoodi — Santo Domingo — 1791+
Ara autochtones — St Croix — Holocene
Ara erythrocephala — Jamaica — 1842
Ara gossei — Jamaica — 1765

Ara guadeloupensis	Guadeloupe Island	1800+
Ara tricolor	Cuba	1885
Aratinga chloroptera maugei	Puerto Rico	1892
Charmosyna diadema	New Caledonia	1880
Conuropsis carolinensis carolinensis	North America	1914
Conuropsis carolinensis ludovicianus	North America	1912
Cyanorhamphus novaezelandiae erythropus	New Zealand	1913
Cyanorhamphus novaezelandiae subflavescens	Lord Howe Island	1869
Cyanorhamphus ulietanus	Society Islands	1774
Cyanorhamphus zelandicus	Tahiti	1844
Geopsittacus occidentalis	Australia	1900+
Hapalopsittaca amazonina fuertisi	Colombia	1911
Lophopsittacus mauritanicus	Maurice Island	1638
Mascarinus mascarinus	Réunion and Maurice Islands	1834
Necropsittacus borbonicus	Réunion Island	1600+
Necropsittacus francius	Maurice Island	1650
Necropsittacus rodericanus	Rodriguez Island	1730
Nestor meridionalis productus	Norfolk Island	1851
Psephotus pulcherrimus	Australia	1900+
Psittacula eques	Réunion Island	1750+
Psittacula exsul	Rodriguez Island	1875
Psittacula wardi	Seychelles Islands	1881
Vini sinotoi	Marquesas Islands	Holocene
Vini vidivici	Marquesas Islands	Holocene

STRIGIFORMES
Tytonidae

Tyto cavatica	Puerto Rico	Holocene
Tyto letocarti	New Caledonia	200+
Tyto newtoni	Maurice Island	1700+
Tyto noeli	Cuba	Holocene
Tyto ostolaga	Hispaniola	Holocene
Tyto pollens	Bahamas	Holocene
Tyto sauzieri	Maurice Island	1700+

Strigidae

Athene blewitti	India	1914
Athene cretensis	Crete	Holocene
Athene murivora	Rodriguez Island	1850+
Bubo leguati	Rodriguez Island	1700+
Bubo sinclairi	North America	Holocene
Nynox novaeseelandiae alba	Lord Howe Island	1940
Ornimegalonyx oteroi	Cuba	Holocene
Otus commersoni	Maurice Island	1850
Otus insularis	Seychelles Islands	1900+
Otus rutilus capnodes	Comoro Islands	1890
Sceloglaux albifacies albifacies	New Zealand	1950
Sceloglaux albifacies rufifacies	New Zealand	1889
Speotyto balearica	Balearic Islands	Holocene
Speotyto cunicularia amaura	Antilles	1890
Speotyto cunicularia guadeloupensis	Marie Galante	1890

CAPRIMULGIFORMES
Aegothelidae

Aegotheles novaezelandiae	New Zealand	Holocene
Aegotheles savesi	New Caledonia	1880

Caprimulgidae

Caprimulgus ludovicianus	Ethiopia	1900+
Siphonornis americanus americanus	Jamaica	1859

Cuculidae

Coua delalandei	Madagascar	1920
Geococcyx conklingi	North America	Pleistocene
Nannococcyx psix	St. Helena Island	1502+
Neomorphus geoffroyi maximiliani	Brazil	1932

Alcedinidae

Halcyon myakoensis	Japan	1841

Upupidae

Upupa antaios	St. Helena Island	1502+

Picidae

Campephilus principalis principalis	North America	1972
Celeus immaculatus	Panama	c.1900
Colaptes cafer rufipileus	Guadeloupe Island	1906

PASSERIFORMES
Tyranidae

Anairetes fernandezianus	Juan Fernandez	1917

Acanthizidae

Gerygone igata insularis	Lord Howe Island	1920

Xenicidae

Xenicus longipes stokesi	New Zealand	c.1900
Xenicus longipes variabilis	New Zealand	1965
Xenicus lyalli	New Zealand	1894

Troglodytidae

Thyromanes bewickii brevicaudus	Guadeloupe Island	1892
Troglodytes aedon mesoleucus	Sainte Lucie	1892

Turdidae

Phaeornis obscurus lainaiensis	Lanai, Hawaii	1931
Phaeornis obscurus oahensis	Oahu, Hawaii	1825
Phaeornis obscurus rutha	Molokai, Hawaii	1936
Turdus ulientensis	Ra'iatea	1780
Turdus xanthopus vinitinctus	Lord Howe Island	1920
Zoothera terrestris	Bonin Islands	1828

Sylviidae

Acrocephalus familiaris familiaris	Laysan	1920
Bowdleria rufescens	Chatham Islands	1895

Muscicapidae

Pomarea nigra tabuensis	Tonga	c.1800

Dicaeidae

Dicaeum quadricolor	Cebu Island (Philippines)	1906

EXTINCT SPECIES

Zosteropidae		
Zosterops semiflava	Seychelles Islands	c.1900
Zosterops strenua	Lord Howe Island	1923
Meliphagidae		
Anthornis melanocephalus	Chatham Islands	1906
Chaetoptila augustipluma	Hawaii	1850
Moho apicalis	Hawaii	1837
Moho nobilis	Hawaii	1934
Moho bishopi	Hawaii	1904
Emberizidae		
Embernagra longicauda	Bahia Island	c.1900
Geospiza nebulosa	Galapagos Islands	c.1850
Loxigilla portoricensis grandis	Puerto Rico	c.1900
Pipilo maculatus consobrinus	Guadeloupe Island	c.1900
Parulidae		
Vermivora bachmanii	North America	c.1950
Drepanididae		
Ciridops anna	Hawaii	1892
Drepanis funerea	Molokai, Hawaii	1907
Drepanis pacifica	Hawaii	1898
Dysmerodrepanis munroi	Lanai, Hawaii	1800+
Hemignathus lucidus affinis	Maui, Hawaii	1896
Hemignathus lucidus hanapepe	Kauai, Hawaii	1965
Hemignathus lucidus lucidus	Oahu, Hawaii	1890
Hemignathus obscurus ellisianus	Oahu, Hawaii	1840
Hemignathus obscurus lainaiensis	Lanai, Hawaii	1894
Hemignathus obscurus obscurus	Hawaii	1940
Hemignathus obscurus procerus	Kauai, Hawaii	1965
Himatione sanguinea freethi	Hawaii	1925
Loxioides flaviceps	Hawaii	c.1800
Loxioides kona	Hawaii	1894
Loxioides palmeri	Hawaii	c.1800
Loxops coccinea rufa	Oahu, Hawaii	c.1900
Loxops maculata flammea	Hawaii	1970
Loxops maculata montana	Lanai, Hawaii	1937
Viridonia sagittirostris	Hawaii	c.1900
Icteridae		
Quiscalus palustris	Mexico	c.1900
Fringillidae		
Acanthis johannis	Somalia	c.1900
Neospiza concolor	Sao Tome	c.1900
Estrildidae		
Estrilda thomensis	Sao Tome	c.1900
Ploceidae		
Foudia bruante	Réunion Island	1776
Sturnidae		
Aplonis corvina	Kusaie Island	1827
Aplonis fuscus hullianus	Lord Howe Island	1925
Aplonis mavornata	Society Islands	1780
Cassidix palustris	Mexico	c.1900
Fregilupus varius	Réunion Island	1868
Necropsar leguati	Rodriguez Island	1840
Callaeidae		
Heteralocha acutirostris	New Zealand	1907

MAMMALS

MARSUPIALS

Macropodiidae		
Bettongia gaimardi	Australia	1900+
Lagorchestes leporides	Australia	1890
Potorous gilberti	Australia	1850+
Potorous platyops	Australia	1900+
Wallabia greyi	Australia	1900+
Peramelidae		
Perameles myosura myosura	Australia	1900+
Perameles fasciata	Australia	1900+
Chaeropus ecaudatus	Australia	1920
Macrotis lagotis grandis	Australia	1930
Dasyuridae		
Antechinus apicalis	Australia	1900+
Thylacinidae		
Thylacinus cynocephalus	Australia	1961

INSECTIVORES

Nesophontidae		
Nesophontes edithae	Puerto Rico	1930
Nesophontes hypomicrus	Antilles	1930
Nesophontes longirostris	Antilles	1930
Nesophontes micrus	Antilles	1930
Nesophontes paramicrus	Antilles	1930
Nesophontes zamicrus	Hispaniola	1930
Solenodon cubanus	Antilles	1910
Soricidae		
Crocidura fuliginosa trichura	Indian Ocean (Christmas Island)	1900
Nesiotites corsicanus	Corsica	Holocene
Nesiotites hidalgo	Balearic Islands	Holocene
Nesiotites similis	Sardinia	Holocene
Thyrrhenicola hanceni	Corsica and Sardinia	Holocene

CHIROPTERA

Phyllostomatidae		
Monophyllus plethodon frater	Puerto Rico	1850
Phyllonycteris obtusa	Hispaniola	1900
Phyllonycteris major	Puerto Rico	1850
Phyllops vetus	Cuba	c.1750
Reithronycteris aphylla	Jamaica	c.1900
Sternoderma rufum	Puerto Rico	1812
Natalidae		
Natalus primus	Cuba	c.1850

PRIMATES

Lemuridae		
Cheirogalus trichotis	Indian Ocean (Christmas Island)	c.1900

Lemur macaco flavifrons	Madagascar	c.1900
Megaladapis (3 species)	Madagascar	c.1600

LAGOMORPHES

Prolagus sardus	Corsica and Sardinia	Holocene

RODENTS

Sciuridae

Epixerus ebii	Liberia	c.1900

Cricetidae

Oryzomys antillarum	Jamaica	1880
Oryzomys victus	Atlantic Ocean (St Vincent)	c.1900

Muridae

Rhagamys orthodon	Corsica and Sardinia	Holocene
Canaryomys bravoi	Canary Islands	Holocene
Canaryomys tamarani	Canary Islands	Holocene
Rattus culmorum austrinus	Australia (Kangaroo Island)	c.1850
Rattus macleari	Indian Ocean (Christmas Island)	c.1900
Rattus nativitatis	Indian Ocean	c.1900

Gliridae

Hypnomys morpheus	Balearic Islands	Holocene

Capromyidae

Geocapromys brownii thoracatus	Jamaica	c.1950
Geocapromys colombianus	Cuba	1850
Geocapromys ingrahami irrectus	Atlantic Ocean (Crooked Island)	c.1600
Geocapromys ingrahami abaconis	Great Abaco Island (Bahamas)	c.1600
Aphaetraeus montanus	Hispaniola	c.1600
Hexolobodon phenex	Hispaniola	c.1600
Isolobodon levir	Haiti	c.1550
Isolobodon portoricensis	Puerto Rico	1700
Plagiodonta spelaeum	Hispaniola	c.1750

Echymyidae

Brotomys offella	Cuba	1870
Brotomys torrei	Cuba	1870
Boromys contractus	Hispaniola	c.1650
Boromys voratus	Hispaniola	c.1650
Heteropsomys insulans	Puerto Rico	c.1750
Homopsomys antillensis	Puerto Rico	c.1750
Megalomys audreyae	Antilles	c.1600
Megalomys demarestii	Antilles	1902
Megalomys luciae	Antilles	1851
Heptaxodon bidens	Puerto Rico	c.1600
Elasmodontomys obliquus	Puerto Rico	c.1600

CARNIVORES

Canidae

Canis lupus hodophylax	Japan	1900+
Canis lupus alces	Alaska	1915
Canis lupus beothocus	Greenland	1900+
Canis lupus mogollonensis	North America	1920
Canis lupus monstrabilis	North America	c.1920
Canis lupus nubilus	North America	1926
Canis lupus youngi	North America	1940
Canis lupus niger	North America	1900+
Canis lupus floridanus	North America	1917
Canis lupus rufus	North America	1970
Dusicyon australis	Atlantic (Malines)	1800+
Sinotherium sardus	Sardinia	Holocene
Vulpes macrotis macrotis	North America	c.1800

Ursidae

Ursus arctos crowtheri	North Africa	1870
Ursus arctos nelsoni	North America	1968
Ursus arctos pescator	Kamchatka	1920

Mustelidae

Mustela macrodon	Canada	1880

Viverridae

Viverra megaspila civettina	India	1967

Felidae

Felis concolor couguar	North America	1900+
Felis onca arizonensis	North America	1905
Panthera leo barbarus	North Africa	1922
Panthera leo melanochaitus	South Africa	1865
Panthera leo persica	Greece	Holocene
Panthera pardus jarvisi	Sinai	1967
Panthera tigris balica	Bali	1937

PINNIPEDS

Otariidae

Zalophus californianus japonicus	Japan	1960

Phocidae

Monachus tropicalis	Antilles	1974

PROBOSCIDIENS

Elephantidae

Elephas falconeri	Sicily	Holocene
Elephas primigenius	Europe	Holocene

SIRENIENS

Dugongidae

Hydrodamalis gigas	North Pacific	1767

PERISSODACTYLES

Equidae

Equus asinus atlanticus	North Africa	Holocene
Equus ferus (tarpan)	Asia	1887
Equus hemionus hemippus	Syria and Iran	1927
Equus quagga	South Africa	1878

EXTINCT SPECIES

Hippopotamidae
Hippopotamus sp.	Sicily	Holocene
Hippopotamus (2 species)	Madagascar	Holocene

ARTIODACTYLES
Cervidae
Candiacervus rethymnensis	Crete	Holocene
Candiacervus ropalophorus	Crete	Holocene
Capra pyrenaica pyrenaica	Pyrenees	1910
Cervus canadensis canadensis	Canada	1800+
Cervus canadensis merriami	North America	1906
Cervus elaphus yarkandensis	Asia	1927
Cervus schomburgki	Thailand	1900+
Megaceros cazioti	Corsica and Sardinia	Holocene

Rangifer dawsoni	Canada	1908
Rangifer tarandus groenlandicus	Greenland	1950

Bovidae
Alcelaphus buselaphus buselaphus	Algeria and Atlas Mountains	1923
Alcelaphus buselaphus caama	South Africa	1940
Bison bison oregonus	North America	1800+
Bison bison pennsylvanicus	North America	1825
Bison bonasus caucasicus	Europe	1930
Bos primigenius	Europe	1627

INDEX